Travels & Travails Across Africa

Michael Marnell

Bestread
Publications

First edition: January 2024

Travels & Travails Across Africa
by Michael Marnell

Cover: Bappaditya

Layout: Sabyasachi Datta

Contact: +91-6291538319, bestread.publications@gmail.com

Published by Dibyendu Ghosh on behalf of Bestread Publications and Digital Services Private Limited
51/C/2/D/4, Chaulpatti Road
Kolkata - 7000 010

To my children Alex and Maddy who
inspired me to finally put pen to paper
& my parents Dixie and Bernie without whom
none of these memories would have been possible!

Prologue

How It All Began

One day, I sat down to complete one of those online surveys where you mark off all the countries you've visited on a world map. When the results showed up, I was astonished to see that my score amounted to ninety countries! Maybe I shouldn't have been all that surprised, however, given the fact that I had lived in, visited, and worked in numerous countries both as a child and an adult over the past fifty-eight years. Having seen such a unique and diverse world out there, I felt that it would be worth recalling some of the more interesting travels and travails that I had experienced across Africa. But how did it all begin?

My late father, Richard, was one of twelve—six boys and six girls—raised on a farm in Kilkenny, Ireland. He trained as a mechanic and by his late twenties was working in Drogheda, County Louth. However, in 1956, he made a decision that would change his life forever and see him leave Ireland for a better life abroad. It was a decision that many of his generation, and generations before him, had taken.

My father, however, didn't head for the usual destinations of the Irish diaspora—the UK, America,

Australia, New Zealand, or Canada. Instead, he joined the United Nations (UN) and began a new life in the Middle East. I never knew the circumstances of how this came about but had always assumed that his decision to leave had been driven by the dire economic circumstances in Ireland at that time.

It was only relatively recently, after my father had passed away, that I learnt the real story of how the opportunity to join the UN came about for him.

Ireland only became a member of the United Nations in December 1955, ten years after the end of the Second World War. In October 1956, the Suez Crisis broke out following the nationalisation of the Suez Canal by Gamal Abdel Nasser, President of Egypt. The Suez Canal was a key route for oil shipments to Europe and was owned by British and French interests. The Israeli army, learning from its experiences in the 1948 war, took this opportunity to push into Egypt to protect its own tenuous borders and support the British and French troops dispatched to retake the Canal. A ceasefire was called following pressure from the Soviet Union and the United States to cease hostilities. To maintain the ceasefire and supervise the withdrawal of the foreign troops, the UN was asked to provide an international peacekeeping force based in the Sinai and Gaza. None of the big powers of the day were asked to contribute forces; rather, the UN looked to non-aligned and neutral countries to fulfil the role.

The UN peacekeeping force comprised troops from Sweden, Denmark, Norway, Finland, Canada, Brazil, Yugoslavia, and India. The mission, called UNEF I (United Nations Emergency Force I) required administration, logistics, security, and transport civilian staff to support the mission. The UN recognised that it would need English speakers, to fill many of these positions. Ireland, a neutral country, was an obvious country to approach. An advertisement was placed in the Irish newspapers looking for the relevant personnel. I don't know how or where my father came across the advertisement, but he applied and was accepted for the Transport Section as a Field Service Officer. Quite a few Irish policemen were also recruited. One of my father's former colleagues, at the time a policeman or Gardai, recalled how he went from sharing a small room in the barracks in Pierce Street in Dublin to a starting salary almost equivalent to that of the Chief of the Irish Police!

In October 1956, my father and his Irish colleagues flew to Tel Aviv to take up their new role with UNEF I based in the Gaza Strip. He subsequently moved in 1967 to the headquarters of UNTSO (United Nations Truce Supervision Organisation) based in Government House in Jerusalem. I can only imagine how he must have felt at the time: a farmer's son, in his twenties, leaving Ireland for the first time and flying to the Holy Land and the exotic lifestyle that lay ahead.

In 1957, my mother, Bernadette, left Ireland to join my father in Jerusalem where they were married in the Old City. Over the course of the next ten years my parents had four children, three boys and a girl, all born in Jerusalem. The eldest, Canice, was born in 1958 on the Israeli side in West Jerusalem. The next, Mark, myself, and then my sister Pamela, were born in East Jerusalem between 1962 and 1968, in the Palestinian side of the city. The city was divided up to 1967, with the Jordanian border running through Jerusalem until the Six Day War in 1967 that saw the whole city come under full Israeli control.

And thus, began the life of an expatriate UN family. A life that would, over the course of the next twenty-seven years, take us from Gaza to Jerusalem, Damascus, Syria, Rawalpindi, Pakistan, Srinagar, Kashmir, Kabul, Afghanistan, Ismailia, Egypt, and finally back to Jerusalem. It would end in 1983 when my mother passed away in Jerusalem after a long fight with cancer. Perhaps it was fate that led us back to where the adventure had begun all those years ago in 1956.

Thirty-five years after my father had boarded that plane in Dublin, I would follow in his footsteps. On Sunday 10 May 1992, I boarded a SABENA aircraft in Brussels; my destination was Kinshasa, Zaïre. It was the start of my own adventure. I was twenty-eight, the same age as my father when he left Ireland in 1956. By another quirk of coincidence, I boarded my flight in Brussels, where my mother had boarded her own flight to Jerusalem thirty-five years ago!

And so began my own travels and travails across Africa.

Contents

PART III

BACK TO THE FUTURE

Part I

The Beating Heart of Conrad

Chapter 1

A New Beginning

As the SABENA 747 descended at dawn towards Ndjili International Airport, Kinshasa, after an overnight flight from Brussels, I wondered what lay in store for me in this mysterious country in the heart of Africa. Only nine months before, Kinshasa had been devastated by riots and looting, leaving much of the city destroyed and with much of its expatriate population having fled the country. And here I was, on 11 May 1992, flying in to take up my new position with the Bank. I had actually volunteered for the role, looking for adventure. To live and work in Zaïre with all its attendant mayhem and insecurity seemed an ideal choice for me. My background of growing up in the UN had played a large part in my decision to move to Kinshasa. I had lived through the Bangladesh Liberation War between India and Pakistan in 1971 when we lived in Rawalpindi and witnessed the aftermath of the Six Day War in 1967 and the Yom Kippur War in 1973 between Israel and its Arab neighbours. I was confident that I would survive this, too.

I was met at the bottom of the aircraft steps by Simon N'Koy holding a placard bearing my name. Simon was the Chef de Protocol (otherwise known as 'Mr Fixit') for the Bank, responsible for obtaining all the government documentation required to live and work in Zaïre: work permit, visa, driving licence. Equally important was his role in ensuring a smooth passage in and out of the airport for us expatriates as well as our general safety around the city.

I was taken to the VIP lounge, where my passport was stamped by immigration and my luggage retrieved from the main terminal. That VIP lounge was an oasis of calm, especially when compared to the chaos of the main airport terminal that I would experience for myself a year later!

Soon we set off for the city. I settled into the back seat of the Range Rover, with Chinois, our driver, and Simon sitting upfront. This wasn't a bad way to start my new life in Zaïre.

The airport is about 40 kms from the city centre. The long ride gave me ample time to absorb the sights, sounds and smells of the city around me. What a bustling place it was! Its population of over seven million far exceeded that of London at the time, and with all the people came all the traffic. And it all seemed to be heading in the same direction as myself! Rush hour, Kinshasa style, was a chaotic mix of overcrowded taxi-vans weaving their way between the slower traffic of heavily overloaded trucks and buses, with the added ingredient of people trying to cross the road without getting run over! Chinois drove with one hand permanently on the horn, warning all in front we were coming through.

After dropping off my bags and freshening up at the Bank's residence situated in the Gombé district of the city, I was taken to the Bank to meet my new colleagues. Over the course of the next few weeks, I settled into the life of an expatriate banker in Kinshasa: working at the bank, finding my way around the city, getting to know those expatriates who had stayed after the riots, meeting interesting Embassy people, and generally immersing myself in the life that the city had to offer. Everyone was very welcoming. It was a wild and unpredictable place and I loved it all! I congratulated myself on making the move from London.

Not long into my new life, Greg, a Canadian friend, offered to take me out one Friday night. He wanted to show me all there was to the city, from the wide variety of restaurants to the lively nightclubs—which ranged from modern western style clubs to local shebeens. We started the evening off with a meal at what would become one of my favourite restaurants, L'Orangerie, on the Boulevard du 30 Juin, the main thoroughfare in the city. Kinshasa was a dangerous place at that time, following the previous year's looting spree, with little law and order to speak of. The foreign community tended to confine themselves to the restaurants, bars and clubs situated within the safer Gombé area of the city, north of the Boulevard. A few hardier souls would venture further south of the Boulevard into the sprawling Cité, the real heart of the city. We were officially advised not to go there given the tense security situation.

A couple of bottles of decent South African wine drunk with dinner, we moved on to explore the various bars and clubs in the area. We pulled up to our final stop very late into the night. I had a rather full bladder at this point and was in urgent need to find a place to relieve myself. The right and proper thing to do, it seemed (to me at least), was to relieve myself in the dark road beside the car; and thus I promptly got down to it. Just as I was finishing, a soldier stepped out of the darkness, rifle slung over his shoulder. His demeanour said that he clearly meant to arrest me for urinating in a public place, even at this late hour! Times were tough in Kinshasa, and there was always someone looking for an opportunity to shake down an unsuspecting victim with a fine—payable in cash!—for violation of some unspecified law or regulation.

Intending to call his bluff, I went to step up onto the sidewalk. Or at least tried to: I only succeeded in catching my foot on the raised curb. And then fell face forward onto the concrete with a sickening thud. It wasn't at that point that the soldier almost dropped his gun and fled, however, but about five seconds later: when I miraculously rebounded—getting back on my feet as if nothing had happened; seemingly no worse for wear for the experience! Clearly the soldier felt there were greater powers at work here and he was best far away from them.

After dusting myself down amid much amusement from my companion Greg, we carried on to the club before calling it a night. I, however, found myself in a fix. Perhaps it was because of the earlier introduction of my skull to the concrete combined with the amount of alcohol consumed—I realised I had no idea where I lived! Greg wasn't going to waste time looking for the house, so we decided that I should crash at his place for the night. Once there, after a final "un pour la route", I was tucked up in the guest bedroom, soundly asleep.

What seemed like a very short time later, I could hear a faint voice calling out my name. It got increasingly louder and more concerned. Slowly I blinked open one bleary eye to find Greg standing over me. Three of his white suited domestiques, his house staff, were standing behind him. They were looking on apprehensively. Everyone breathed a huge sigh of relief as I woke up and asked what was going on. Greg explained he had just got back from work to be greeted by his staff in a state of panic. It was two o'clock in the afternoon and he had arrived home to the grave news, "Patron, le mondelé il e mort!" Boss, the white man is dead!

It turned out that I had not moved in my bed all morning and hadn't responded to the various prods and nudges from the housekeeper in his attempt to wake me. He had therefore concluded that I must be dead! I assured them that I was quite alive and well and rose, Lazarus-like, from my deathbed. A thumping headache gleefully accompanied me, reminding me not only of my encounter with the concrete path the night before, but also the vast amount of wine, beer and gin that I had consumed.

To make matters worse, I hadn't answered my personal radio all morning. We carried Motorola radios for security reasons to keep in contact, as there was no functioning telephone system. My call sign was Delta. Being new to the city and not having returned to my house the previous night, my colleagues were increasingly concerned that I might have been kidnapped or worse, was lying dead somewhere!

After a quick call to reassure everyone that I was still alive and sort of well, it was time to leave and get myself ready for an afternoon of rugby with the Kinshasa Barbarians! Just another Saturday morning hangover before a rugby game after an excellent night out. Some things clearly hadn't been left behind in London!

Chapter 2

Rugby Really is a Matter of Life or Death!

I was by now settled into my new life in Kinshasa. Outside of work, I tried to keep myself active. I had been told, before I moved to Kinshasa, that there was a rugby scene in the city with several local military sides, and a mixed expatriate/local team called the Kinshasa Barbarians. The team had been founded by Bobby, an expatriate from Wales, many years ago when times weren't this rough. They had played in Kinshasa and even across the river in Brazzaville in the days when it was possible to do so. The team was now run by two Americans, Harry, and Greg. Both were the sons of missionary families, born and raised in Zaïre. At various times the nucleus of the team comprised members of the Royal Military Police security protection team from the British Embassy, several former British Army officers contracted as private security to the few multinational companies still based in Kinshasa, some English diamond buyers working for De Beers, and several Frenchmen involved in various local businesses. Over the two years I played for the team, we also had South African and US embassy personnel and an Israeli diamond dealer turn out for a game or two. At one of our games, one of the ex-British army security contractors let slip that he played the bagpipes, which he happened to have in his car. We promptly had him lead us out on to the pitch in a single file while playing the bagpipes. He must have ended up scaring the hell out of the opposition with the racket he was making!

Even though rugby had been played for many years in Kinshasa, thinking back on that time now, I felt that it must have been an intriguing sport for the local population to get their heads around. They may not have understood the game; but the fact that two guys, white or black, could smack each other about on the pitch must have symbolised some form of resistance, particularly against the regime. This sense of resistance was there because, at the time, they risked arrest over much more trivial things when going about their daily business. When the opposition was often a hated military team, it perhaps had even greater resonance.

On one occasion, there was a football match being played on the pitch between two local sides. We were waiting for it to end so that we could play our game. One of the football teams turned out to be from SARM, the military intelligence division. At some point, a fight happened to break out in the middle of the pitch, and suddenly it felt like someone had flipped a switch.

Everyone, including our own rugby players, swarmed across the pitch getting their retaliation in, throwing punches and kicks at the players from SARM. Kick, punch and keep running—that was the way of it. It was a rare moment to witness the people taking out their frustrations on those who oppressed them.

Our own French players often seemed more interested in picking fights with the opposition players than playing. I realised very quickly that I was much better off (and safer) playing in the backs and quickly reinvented myself as a fly half, having previously played hooker or flanker in the forwards. I felt vindicated with my decision during a game when one of the opponents planted his teeth firmly in the forehead of one of the French players, following yet another bust up amongst the forwards! This, after all, was the era of AIDS.

Our rugby games were lively affairs, particularly when we were playing against the military, such as the Division Spéciale Présidentielle, known as the DSP, the Parachute Regiment, or SARM. The DSP answered only to President Mobuto and were trained by the Israeli military. Consisting only of members of Mobuto's tribe, they were the best-equipped unit in the country. They were feared and often deployed to suppress internal dissent. People taken away by them often simply disappeared.

Towards the end of the season, we found ourselves in the semi-final of the Kinshasa Rugby Championship. We didn't even know that there was a Rugby Championship! I thought we were playing for fun! Our opponents were the DSP, and the game was to be played out near the international airport at Ndjili. When we arrived and began to warm up on a very sandy pitch, the local residents began to gather to see what was going on.

The DSP were always a tough opposition to play against. They had a strong team and a talented big number eight forward by the name of Manzikala, so we knew that it would be a hard game. We had managed to cobble together a team of waifs and strays, as many of our regular players were either overseas or unavailable. To make matters worse, the referee was a short overweight Frenchman not known for his impartiality.

As the game kicked off, the locals cheered the DSP, probably more out of a sense of self-preservation than any real sense of loyalty. During the first thirty minutes we found ourselves under pressure and were grimly hanging onto the coattails of the game. Manzikala collected the ball from an attacking scrum inside our 22-metre line, and set off on a barnstorming run targeting the opposition fly half. He proceeded to trample his way over the said player, in the style of Jonah Lomu in his prime, leaving my dignity well and truly buried in the sand to score under the posts. A penalty kick followed soon after, and the Kinshasa Barbarians were suddenly ten points adrift.

Regrouping, we slowly clawed our way back into the game. Against the odds, we scored a try of our own just before the break to reach half time only three points down.

The second half became a tense affair, with the tide of the touchline support slowly swinging over to the Barbarians. The locals, perhaps realising that we were fighting a proxy battle for them, began cheering our every tackle and skirmish with the DSP. Encouraged, we raised our game further. Finally, we had a chance to strike. From an attacking scrum, I told my scrum half to get the ball back to me as quickly as he could. Standing directly behind the scrum, I took his pass and, in a flash, struck the sweetest drop goal ever seen north of the Limpopo. The ball was still rising as it went through the posts, and we were tied at ten points apiece with minutes to go.

With the clock counting down, the referee began awarding penalties to the DSP for various imagined offences. It was now obvious to us that we were not meant to win at the expense of the DSP. Penalty after penalty were awarded, and each time the DSP would go for the kick at goal. And one after another, the ball would sail wide of the uprights. And each time, the touch judges would indicate the kick was wide. Both touch judges happened to be two of our local substitutes.

With time expiring, the referee awarded yet another penalty out wide on the touchline. The DSP kicker stepped up and again sent his kick just wide of the posts. However, as the ball flew past, our two touch judges immediately raised their flags signifying that the kick was in fact good! Stunned, we looked at them and demanded to know what they were doing, as the kick was clearly wide.

Both looked at us sheepishly, shrugged their shoulders, and said, "They know where we live."

As the DSP celebrated their narrow 13-10 victory, we were left to ruminate over the fact that these very same players could that night be kicking in someone's door and dragging them away, for them to be never seen again.

Given the reality of life in Zaïre, it really wasn't worth arguing over something as innocuous as a penalty kick, especially when it was your teammate's very life that was ultimately on the line.

One could only reflect that a game of rugby in Zaïre really was a matter of life or death!

Chapter 3

Fifteen Minutes of Fame

Simon N'Koy, our Chef de Protocol, decided it was time for me to experience the Cité, located south of the Boulevard, in the Matongé Quartier. The area was known for its vibrant music scene and nightlife. Zaïrean music, soukous, was famous across Africa, and the opportunity to experience another aspect of the city was appealing. While officially we were discouraged from going to the Cité at night due to the volatile security situation in Kinshasa, it sounded rather exciting, and with Simon chaperoning me on his home turf, it should be quite safe. Simon lived in Matongé and, apart from his Bank duties, ran a small clothing business from a shop he called the London City Market. The shop sold the second-hand clothes that he would bring back from his annual trip to the UK. Whatever else Simon might be involved in, he was invaluable in ensuring that our day to day lives were made just that little bit easier through his connections and contacts.

Simon had a great sense of humour, and we often

had a good laugh together about one thing or another. For example, he had an air conditioner in his office that he would often leave on when he left at the end of the day. As his office door would be locked, we would have to turn it off through the mains power switch. The next day, he would go into his office and try to turn it on. He would then come into my or my colleague's office and inform us solemnly that his air conditioner was broken. He would suggest that we get an engineer in to fix it. One of us would go over to the power point, flick the switch, and miraculously the air conditioner would spring back into life. Simon would turn to us and with a solemn look, say "Patron, my father always told me, the white man is not as stupid as he looks!" How we laughed! He really was a loveable rogue in many ways.

On the day of my Cité tour, I was collected by my driver and driven to Simon's house. I had brought a bottle of Johnny Walker Red Label as a gift and was looking forward to the experience ahead. On arrival, I was introduced to Simon's extended family and friends, who were sitting out on a little veranda facing the street. Hanging off the railings were about twenty kids intrigued by the sight of a "mondelé" paying a visit! I was introduced to Simon's "brother", his elderly sister, and several of his rather attractive lady friends. Simon told me that his "brother" would be my bodyguard for the evening in case we ran into any trouble when we went out later. Smiling, his "brother" opened his jacket to reveal a pistol tucked into a shoulder holster inside.

We drank cold Primus beer and chatted, with Simon translating my words into the local Lingala dialect, while lively Congolese music played in the background. When I told Simon's elderly sister that I was Irish, she dug out a U2 CD from somewhere and played it without pause while insisting that I dance with her, much to the amusement of the kids hanging off the railings.

Later in the evening, I noticed that the whiskey bottle was empty on the table. Looking around, I discovered my "bodyguard" slumped comatose in a corner, his jacket wide open, with his pistol in the open for all to see. Well, so much for my personal bodyguard tonight!

As midnight approached, Simon decided that it was time for us to head out and experience the local nightlife. Leaving my bodyguard behind, we set off in two cars down dark, rutted streets, finally pulling up outside a nondescript building. I was impressed to find a smart club inside. There was a stage on which a band was playing, a dance floor in front of it, tables and chairs laid around the room, and a bar in the adjoining room. There were only two other "mondelés" in the club that I could tell, sitting at a table in the dark shadows at the back of the club. The band was playing a lively tune, with young couples dancing and enjoying themselves.

We headed to the bar, and after a couple of cold beers, I was finally ready to hit the dance floor—with much encouragement from my companions. I joined the smartly dressed crowd and danced along to the music. Congolese songs are not known for their brevity, seeming to go on forever, so I just danced and danced. I loved it and, having quickly picked up the rhythm of the music, danced well into the early hours of the morning. It was at least 4 am when we called it a night and headed home.

I was dropped back at my apartment in Gombé as the sun was rising—tired, hot, and sweaty, but excited at having experienced what the Cité had to offer.

That Monday morning when I arrived at work, I was greeted by the staff with cries of "patron!" whilst they waved their arms above their heads as if mimicking my dancing. I was puzzled, and called Simon to my office to ask what was going on.

Simon explained that RTZ, the national television station, had been broadcasting live from the nightclub we were in on Saturday night. Apparently, the band was quite famous in Kinshasa. Many of our bank staff would have been sitting at home watching the show when suddenly, out of nowhere, I appeared on their television screens, dancing amongst the crowd! I asked him if he could get a copy of the show, and a couple of days later, he popped into my office and handed over a video cassette of the programme.

That night I watched the show. Picture the scene. The camera is directly opposite the band playing on stage. The crowd is dancing between the camera and the stage. The camera slowly pans from right to left, in a panoramic sweep of the crowd. It passes a sweating white face in the midst of the black crowd, arms raised, pumping the air in time to the music. It comes to a sudden stop and reverses back to the white face in the crowd. And then zooms in for a closer look, as if to confirm to the nation that, yes, that really is a "mondelé" dancing in the middle of the crowd!

And that's how I ended up in everyone's house in Kinshasa that evening! It certainly did my street credibility a lot of good with the staff that week! The show was re-broadcast the following weekend, so of course I was back dancing in their houses that night as well. And again came the whole greeting package, complete with the arm waving, the following Monday!

It was a great evening and experience. Appearing on Zaïrean television, albeit without my knowledge, completed my unique personal experience of having appeared on national television in three different countries, Pakistan, Ireland and now Zaïre!

I had found my fifteen minutes of fame!

Chapter 4

To Live and Work in Kinshasa

The atmosphere in Kinshasa throughout 1992 and in early 1993 was tense. The political and economic crisis in the country following the first Pillage in September 1991 continued. The year before, Zaïrean military units had gone on a weeklong rampage after not getting paid their salaries for months. The civilian population of the city had joined in and devastated the city in an orgy of looting. This ultimately led to Belgian and French troops intervening to evacuate their nationals and help restore order. When order had been restored, and with foreign pressure exerted on President Mobuto, a conference of national sovereignty was convened to address reforming the political and constitutional landscape of the country. The key protagonists in the political standoff at the time were the reformist Prime Minister Etienne Tshisekedi, and the President, Mobuto Sese Seko.

Life for much of the population in Kinshasa was a daily struggle for survival. The economy was in ruins with rampant hyperinflation where prices often changed by the hour. Bizarrely, for such a poor and broken country, Zaïre had a selection of excellent locally brewed beers to choose from, the most popular being Primus. This led me to form my now universally accepted economic theory that "the harsher the quality of life is in a country; the better the quality of its beer": a key ingredient in keeping a population happy despite their circumstances! This certainly seemed true of Zaïre at that time.

The end of every month was always a tense period, as it was never certain if the government had the money to pay the military. History had shown that if the military didn't get paid, it took, as happened the previous year. I recall being told of the events of 1991 by those who were there at the time. The population had engaged in a frenzy of looting and swarmed through the wealthier Mbinza and Gombé districts, taking everything that they could. And I do mean everything. This included stripping houses down to their bare concrete shells. Anything that could be ripped from a wall or floor, such as tiling, wiring, and electrical sockets, had a value to the looters. A prominent expatriate businessman told me a great story of how he and his wife had run from their house and hidden under a blanket in the bushes in their garden as the mob swarmed over the walls of his property like ants. Watching as their possessions and treasured family heirlooms were being carried away, he whispered to his wife that if this had been in a Wilbur Smith novel, they would be making mad passionate love at that moment. To which his wife apparently told him where to go; in no uncertain terms! I admired his sense of humour at such a difficult and dangerous moment; it was the sort of thing I might have said!

With that background in mind, as each month's end approached, we not only had to pay salaries but also find fifty-two sacks of rice and coffee for our local staff. With inflation rampant in the country, the local currency, the Zaïre, had rapidly depreciated from Z200,000 to the US Dollar in May 1992, when I had arrived in Kinshasa, to Z9,000,000 to the US Dollar by January 1993. Shops no longer listed prices on goods but merely displayed a number. You simply checked the number of a particular item against a list of prices on a blackboard above the entrance for the latest price. Within the hour that price could change, and by the end of the day, be significantly more expensive than it was at the beginning.

Everything in Kinshasa revolved around cash. Bills were paid in cash, salaries were paid in cash, goods were paid for in cash. Credit cards were redundant, and cheques were purely used for specific intra-account transactions. There was a separate exchange rate applicable to each type of transaction, be it cash or cheque, local currency or foreign. Cash, however, was king. Cheques could be paid into a bank account, but you couldn't then withdraw the cash equivalent for it. There simply wasn't enough withdrawable cash. Cash was a rare commodity, and Kinshasa was very much a cash economy. We had to struggle continuously to upgrade our IT system, for it to accommodate the additional zeros appearing on bank statements to account for the rapidly devaluing currency. At the time, our IT Help Desk was in Bangalore, India; regular and expensive satellite phone calls seeking help had to be made to them. My first monthly gross salary payment amounted to Z454,952,261, making me an instant multi-millionaire at the age of twenty-eight! Even after 50% tax I was getting paid Z227,473,680. Unfortunately, it didn't buy me a Ferrari or that apartment in Monaco! It only amounted to about USD 1,000!

Eating out in Kinshasa was a wonderful experience. There were a number of excellent restaurants in the city, from the high end and expensive Le Caf'Conc to the more "affordable" places, such as my personal favourites, L'Orangerie and Chez Nicola. The cuisine on offer in the city catered to all tastes—whether it be French, Italian, Lebanese, Chinese, Greek, Indian or Zaïrean—with even a good old US burger and fries available from the US Embassy sports club. Going out to eat entailed carrying a bag or briefcase loaded with bricks of cash. Each brick comprised twenty-five banknotes. At the end of a meal, everyone would place their bricks on the table for the waiter to collect. He would load them on a tray and head off to count them: a scene more reminiscent of Berlin in the 1920s, perhaps!

Life in Kinshasa was a whole galaxy away from the life I had known back in London. Most of the things I had taken for granted there were no longer available in my new world. This was long before mobile phones, emails and the internet were even heard of. Landline telephones were useless, as the infrastructure simply wasn't there. The only quick and efficient means of communication was to have a satellite phone. These phones were about the size of a brick, and were an essential fashion item for any self-respecting businessman or politician in town. It was the only way to conduct business in Kinshasa and for us to keep in contact with our Head Office and families overseas. As a result, many deals were concluded in Kinshasa over these phones, and nowhere did the phrase "Your word is your bond" hold truer than in Kinshasa at that time.

When you compare mobile tariffs today, it's incredible to think making international calls was an absolute luxury, at a cost of over USD 7 per minute. My phone calls back to London were generally limited to once a week, usually on a Sunday evening.

Within the Bank, we each had a Motorola radio, or "walkie-talkie", which allowed us to keep in contact with one another when moving about the city. In addition, there was a warden radio system in place run by the British Embassy, through which they could alert British nationals in the event of any sudden trouble in the city. So, despite the lack of telephones, we had the means to remain in contact at all times.

Driving around the city, you were regularly stopped at a crossroads or junction by the Guarde Civile, a paramilitary police unit, for some perceived driving offence. If you handed over your documents for inspection, you were likely to end up paying a "fine" to get them back. I was offered a very useful tip from an old hand, Lynda: that I should carry photocopies of my driving licence and identity documents rather than the originals. Handing over these photocopies and losing them was much more convenient than the originals, and saved you the trouble of needing to get them back! The Guarde Civile could be a pain when moving around town, and I was always a little nervous when I saw them hanging around as I approached a junction. The trick was to look confident and disinterested as you passed by. There were always two of them stationed at the main crossroads on the drive from my apartment to the bank, and there was no real way of avoiding them. In the end, we decided that it was just easier to have someone provide them with a petit cadeau—a little gift—every month, rather than run the daily gauntlet. From then on, they were our Guarde Civile, and always gave us a smart salute and a nod as we drove past—even whilst in the process of shaking down their latest victim!

Another major hurdle that we faced was finding enough petrol to keep the bank vehicles on the road. Petrol was in constant short supply, which meant that when any became available, long queues would form, more in hope than any real expectation. Indeed, just a rumour that petrol was available at a certain station was enough to cause a queue. Cars would be pushed along the line to save what petrol they already had. The petrol queue created an industry of car minders—people who looked after cars left in the queue by owners, for a fee. The owner would walk to work whilst the carer would push it forward to fill it in due course, until the owner returned later in the day. A few more enterprising souls could be found along the sides of the road, selling plastic containers full of petrol for a steep price. These chaps were known as Gaddafis—in honour of the Libyan leader. Despite these shortages, our staff performed miracles in ensuring that our cars always had enough petrol.

Kinshasa had many attractions other than restaurants, bars, nightclubs and rugby to keep me busy. There was a weekly volleyball night at the American School, where our Cowbell team was a particularly inept but willing participant. There was an attempt at running a Hash House Harriers social running club in the city, but it raised suspicions amongst the locals as to why expatriates were driving around, marking the route on the roads with chalk. Initially, the organisers had tried to use shredded paper piles, but these were taken as soon as they were left behind. Given the sensitivity of the authorities, chalk marking the route could very quickly lead to accusations of spying, so the Harriers died out rather quickly.

I also played doubles tennis once a week with an eclectic mix of partners: the Israeli ambassador, the Papal Nuncio, and my good friends Bobby, Nicky, Greg and Lynda.

There was even an eighteen-hole golf course located right in the centre of the city. We even played the first ever Ryder Cup at the Kinshasa Golf Club!

My favourite tournament was sponsored by the local Heineken-owned brewery. This consisted of a cross-country golf competition, where you played from the first tee to the third green, and so on. A beer truck would drive around the course as you played, and for every small glass of beer drunk, you received a token. For every token in your possession at the end of the round, you had a shot deducted from your final score. The more beer you drank, of course, the more shots you took! Quite a few golfers staggered off the 18th green, clutching his or her tokens as a badge of honour. I would know; I was one of them!

The highlight of the week, however, was to head to the Club Nautique on a Sunday morning. People kept speedboats there, and every Sunday, they would head out on to the mighty Zaïre River for the day. The Zaïre or Congo River is very fast-flowing, with a powerful set of rapids, known as the Livingston Falls, located just to the west of the city. The accepted practice was to head out on the river in pairs, just in case one boat broke down in the middle of Stanley Pool. The Pool (or Pool Malebo as it is now known) is twenty-two miles long and fourteen miles wide, so it could feel like you were in the middle of the sea rather than on a river. If you broke down, your boat could be swept towards the rapids at an alarming pace; so another boat was always extremely helpful, and a welcome tow home. And breakdowns were a regular occurrence. From what I had been told, no one had ever survived the rapids—even those who had willingly attempted them.

We would travel upriver in convoy for some distance until we found a suitable sandbank or beach to pitch camp for the day. During the dry season, the river could be quite shallow, so one had to be careful not to steer the boat into a submerged sandbank along the way. Once anchors were dropped, the group would settle down for the day under the shade of a gazebo. There was always a very competitive game of boules played on the sand, and occasionally, someone might go for a spot of water skiing. Given the heat of the day, the best option was often to sit in the shallows of the great river with a glass of beer or wine in hand to cool down. There was no risk of crocodiles in the water this far downriver, due to the high rate of flow of the river —or so we believed anyway! The biggest risk to our bodies came from other unseen little devils lurking in the water.

I learnt this the hard way early on in my time in Kinshasa, as on one such outing, I sat in the shallow pitch-black water with a beer in hand. I suddenly felt a sharp sting on my chest and jumped up out of the water as quickly as I could! I looked at where I had felt the sting, and found a neat round hole where a mole had once been. It had been plucked clean off! It turned out that there were little fish in the water that were attracted to anything on your bare skin that looked appetising, such as moles. To counter these biting fish, everyone wore t-shirts in the water—a practice that I quickly adopted myself! It's funny how, thirty years later, you can now pay for the pleasure of sticking your feet in a basin full of little fish to have them nibble away at all the dead skin. In the Congo River, one could have the full treatment free of charge courtesy of those little fish—although perhaps in a way more extreme than desirable!

The Congo River on a Sunday was a great way to entertain visitors to the city, even if they were unintended ones. On one occasion, I was asked by the British Embassy if I could look after two British journalists, Miles Bredin and Harriet Logan, for a few days. They had been in Angola working on a story for a UK national newspaper about the Benguela Railway Line, which they were going to follow from Angola all the way to Mozambique. After the Angolan elections in 1992, civil war had broken out again in Luanda and they had been evacuated to Kinshasa at short notice. The two spent a week with me before they headed off to Lubumbashi in the south to pick up the trail of the railway line again. During their time with me, they enjoyed everything Kinshasa had to offer. On their last Sunday in town, I took them out on the river with our usual gang, where they enjoyed our hospitality for the day.

In 1995, I had returned to London after my posting to Zaïre had ended. One day, I was browsing in the travel book section of a bookshop when I came across a book titled "Blood on the Tracks: A Rail Journey from Angola to Mozambique" by Miles Bredin, with pictures by Harriet Logan! These were the very same journalists who had stayed with me in Kinshasa three years previously. I bought the book and was delighted to find that there was a substantial section devoted to their time spent in Kinshasa. Several people I knew were mentioned in it. There was even a reference on page 83 to "Mike, who worked for Grindlays Bank". That was me!

Fame at last! I thought. Whilst the chapter about Zaïre went on to describe the hardship of daily life in Kinshasa for both expatriates and the local populace alike, I felt it was a little too sensational in its portrayal compared to my own recollections of my time in the city.

In 1993, or possibly in early 1994, I was also asked to look after a young journalist who was starting a new posting in Kinshasa for Reuters. She was called Michela Wrong, and she subsequently published a book about the Congo in 2000 called In the Footsteps of Mr Kurtz. Sadly, I did not feature in that one!

Our lazy Sundays on the river would end late in the afternoon with a slow leisurely sail back to the Club Nautique. We would aim to be back before dark for safety reasons, but would stop in the Pool for a final beer as the sun began to set spectacularly over the city.

To spend a day on the Congo River was to spend a day washing away the stress and strain of our daily lives in the city; for one day in the week we enjoyed the peace and quiet of our surroundings, until the whole process was repeated the following week. It was our version of Groundhog Day!

Chapter 5

The Second Pillage

I had now been living in Kinshasa for nine months and had settled into the rhythm of the city. Life carried on despite the worsening political and security situation in the city and the country generally. When I had arrived in May 1992, a conference of national sovereignty had been convened to try and draw up a new constitution and organise new elections. It had been born out of the riots that rocked the city the previous year. This was a sign of concession by the President that change in some form was needed. The proceedings, chaired by the head of the Catholic Church, were broadcast live on national radio daily for the benefit of the population. Our staff listened intently every day to the proceedings on the radio, often with much hilarity at the posturing of the politicians. Whether change would be real or imagined was yet to be determined, given the wily machinations of President Mobutu Sese Seko, well versed in playing his opponents off against each other. If he wasn't throwing them in prison one day, he was offering them the role of a Minister the next. Nothing in Kinshasa was ever quite as it seemed, and tensions continued to bubble just under the surface.

Overhanging the whole process was the ever-present threat that the military would not get paid at the end of each month. To keep the military happy and thus prevent a repeat of the First Pillage in 1991, the President needed to find the cash to pay them. With the economy in ruins, his solution was simply to mint more money. By December 1992, rumours were circulating throughout the city that a new bank note, a five million denomination, had been imported to pay the military.

Things were tense as I spent my first Christmas and New Year in Kinshasa. As we moved into the new year of 1993, I was planning my next visit back to the UK at the end of the month. I had booked myself on the SABENA evening flight to Brussels on the 29th, and was looking forward to heading home for a couple of weeks' holiday. With rumours continuing to circulate in the city about the military and the potential new banknotes, it just might be a good time to be out of the country.

On the Thursday morning of the 28th, we were in the office when we heard that the new five million banknotes had been issued to pay the army. However, at the same time, the Prime Minister, Etienne Tshisekedi, had gone on national radio and decreed that these new banknotes were not legal tender and should not be accepted. As a result, the market traders refused to accept the new notes from the soldiers.

Finding that no one would accept their money, the soldiers did the next best thing, which was to take what they wanted at gunpoint, unleashing a storm of looting, destruction and killing across the city.

The new banknotes were not accepted anywhere in the country except in Mobutu's home province of Equateur and in Katanga province in the south. This in turn created an immediate black market for the notes and an opportunity for exchange rate arbitrage for canny traders in Kinshasa. They would buy the unwanted notes in the city and fly them down to Lubumbashi in Katanga, and exchange them there. It was a dangerous game, however; to be caught with the new notes was to invite a harsh reprisal from the authorities.

We continued working in the bank that morning, until the silence of the day was shattered by the sound of heavy gunfire ringing out across the city. Simon had been keeping in touch with his local contacts and informed us that the soldiers had started looting the markets. We decided that it would be best to close the bank and send our staff home. We packed our Toyota Landcruiser with as many as could fit in, and sent them on their way. Thankfully, everyone made it home, although we never saw that Landcruiser again! The official story given was that it had been stolen by the military, although it is entirely possible that one of the staff had taken advantage of the situation to sell it and claim that it was stolen. Either way, we were never to see it again.

And thus, the Second Pillage had begun. And I was definitely not going to be flying home the next day!

As the looting gathered momentum, the opportunity arose for more sinister elements in the military to take advantage of the situation to settle personal scores and to target specific opposition politicians and businessmen and their properties. It was later estimated that somewhere between 300 to 1,000 people were killed over the four-day-long wave of violence. Thankfully, all those that I knew remained relatively unscathed in person, although many had their businesses looted and destroyed. I recall one businessman telling me how he had resisted a mob trying to break in the gates to his factory. He had his staff fire off a few shots with some old rifles to scare the mob off. After a couple of attempts to break in, things went quiet for a few minutes until the mob returned. He had another round of shots fired over the gate, but this time, a tremendous volley of shots from heavy weapons came back from the other side. He realised that there was no way he could stop the mob getting in, especially now that they too were armed. He ordered his staff to flee and find somewhere to hide within the premises. The comedic moment, if there could be one in such a situation, was that every time he found a spot to hide himself, there was already one of his staff hiding there who would shoo him away. Eventually, he found a safe place to hide that wasn't already taken, and stayed unharmed while the mob ransacked the property.

On a more sombre note, we heard that afternoon that the French Ambassador, Philippe Bernard, had been shot and killed in his office, apparently whilst holding a meeting with Prime Minister Tshisekedi. Although later officially attributed to a stray bullet fired during the looting, the commonly accepted fact was that it was an assassination attempt on the Prime Minister.

Back at the bank, my colleague Peter and I locked up the premises. The two of us and Simon remained at the bank with a few soldiers standing guard at the barred gates. They had been provided by one of our customers, General Mahelé, the Zaïrean Army Chief of Staff. In 1997, he would be shot and killed by President Mobutu's son for advocating a peaceful handover of Kinshasa to Laurent Kabila's invading troops rather than risk a civilian bloodbath while defending the city.

With nothing better to do and it being too unsafe to venture out on the streets, Peter and I sat in the staff bar located in the backyard. We drank beer and played a little table tennis whilst monitoring our radios for news of events outside. Our only means of communication to the outside world was our satellite phone, our Motorola radios for use within Kinshasa, and the British Embassy radio kept for events such as this.

As things settled down briefly later that afternoon, we thought that it might be prudent to send a car led by a soldier over to Peter's house, which was nearby, to rescue his dog and a German friend, Sabina who was staying there, and bring them back to the safety of the Bank. With both rescued, we settled in for a potentially long night ahead, waiting for news of what was going on around the city.

Eventually, one of the British Embassy staff called

us on the warden radio to see whether we were safe and had sufficient food and water.

I answered the call and replied, "Yes, we are all fine. As far as food is concerned, we have the German girl and the dog with us, but we aren't sure which one we will eat first!"

The silence at the other end told me that perhaps I wasn't taking the situation as seriously as I should.

After several hours, things appeared to have calmed down enough for us to decide that it would be better to make a dash to my apartment rather than stay at the bank. My apartment was in a reasonably secure location in Gombé, about half a mile away from the bank, flanked on one side by the US Embassy sports club and on the other by the French Embassy residence. Peter, Sabina and I and our dog squeezed into the back seat of our one remaining car, with two armed soldiers sitting up front. We set off from the bank with the car lights off. Thankfully, we didn't encounter any trouble along the way.

At the apartment complex, we decided that it would be safer to stay in an apartment in the block next to mine. A friend of ours lived there, and his company provided security to the multinational companies and embassies in Kinshasa. Staying with him would keep us better informed on the evolving situation, given his network of contacts around the city. We spent the next two nights sitting in the balcony of his apartment on the ninth floor, with all the lights off, watching machine gun tracer fire crisscross the city skyline in a bizarre and deadly firework-like display.

Rival army units had begun to turn on each other after a curfew had been put in place from dusk to dawn. Occasionally, we would quietly move indoors as we spotted groups of soldiers moving through the neighbourhood below. There was no point in drawing attention to ourselves.

To my amazement, the next day, my domestique turned up at the gate to the complex. Theo was at least sixty years of age and a man I owed much to. He kept me fed and watered every day, kept my apartment spotless, and more importantly, was the guardian at the gate who never let anyone into my apartment on a Saturday morning, knowing full well that the Patron had been out late the night before. To have turned up in the middle of the looting in the city at such great risk to himself was beyond the call of duty.

He explained that he had unplugged my fridge the previous day to defrost it in anticipation of my departure on vacation, and had come back to plug it back in. I told him to take whatever he needed and get home quickly before the curfew. I last saw him heading off with a bag of meat under each arm and wished him safe passage on his way.

By Sunday, things had begun to calm down as some form of order was slowly restored across the city. After the death of the French Ambassador, the French Government had placed troops across the river in Brazzaville, preparing to cross the river to evacuate its nationals. We heard that Belgian troops were also in Brazzaville, but the Zaïrean Government made it clear that they would not be welcome in Kinshasa, which was not surprising given the long and difficult history between the two nations.

That morning, the British Embassy called us on the radio and asked if we had any British nationals looking to join an evacuation that was being organised. If so, they should meet at a muster point at the Belgian Embassy. My colleague Peter took the call and confirmed there was one British national for evacuation—myself. On informing Peter that I was in fact an Irish national, he corrected himself, whereupon the Embassy promptly replied that I should go to the French Embassy residence instead! I laughed, thinking that this was probably their payback for my flippant response days earlier!

I walked across to the French Embassy residence on the other side of the road. The compound was crammed full of French, Belgian, Greek, British, Portuguese and Indian nationals who had sought refuge there. Many had been forced to flee their homes in the very clothes they were wearing. The lucky ones had managed to hurriedly pack a few belongings in a suitcase. My nostrils were assaulted by the foul stench from the toilets that had clearly stopped working. I couldn't imagine what it must have been like to have spent the last three days in such conditions. Several of them looked shell-shocked at the swift turn of events which had destroyed livelihoods for many. I found a familiar face there, an engineer from Manchester who had been visiting a local textiles factory to install new equipment and had only been in town for a month. All he had been able to take with him was his briefcase!

After some time, a convoy of trucks pulled up outside, and we were instructed to get on board. We were to be driven to the port which the French paratroopers had secured, having crossed over that morning. As I climbed up into the last truck, one of our customers came running up to me and handed me a bunch of USD cheques that he wanted deposited into his company account in London. This was premium customer service: the Bank was still open, and the Bank was me sitting in the back of a truck!

The port was a short drive away. We were directed towards a ferry preparing to depart for Brazzaville. The ferry was already packed with families and their meagre belongings. Half an hour later we were docking in Brazzaville, where we were met by local immigration officials. We were relieved of our passports and moved towards a line of waiting buses. We were driven to a local school where a few desks had been placed around a sports field, each displaying a national flag for those evacuated. For the next seven hours we milled around, waiting for something to happen as night fell. Eventually, we were instructed to go to our respective country desks, where temporary visas would be issued for entry into the country.

As one of only two Irishmen in Kinshasa that I knew of, I assumed that my passport would be at the UK desk and I headed over to find it. It turned out not to be there, and so I began to wander from desk to desk in the hope of finding it. I went to the Indian desk, which had a big group of Indian nationals waiting patiently beside it.

On the table was a large pile of Indian passports stacked up to one side, and sitting on its own beside them was my Irish passport! An official had an old ledger open in front of him and was just about to take the first Indian passport off the pile to record the details in it by hand. Realising that it would take quite some time before he finally got to my passport, I forced my way to the front and quickly drew his attention to the single Irish passport, suggesting that perhaps it might make more sense to start with that one first. To my relief he agreed, picked up my passport, leafed through the pages—and then asked why I was even there! He informed me that I already had a visa in my passport to enter the country and I was free to leave! It was now over eight hours since we had arrived in Brazzaville, but I felt lucky to be able to walk out, knowing that the others would be there for many more hours to come.

A couple of my British friends working in the diamond business had remained in Kinshasa and they had asked their colleagues in Brazzaville to offer me a place to stay until I could get a flight out of the country. I was collected from the school, and we headed into the city for an excellent steak dinner washed down with a fine bottle of red wine. By the end of the night, I settled into a comfortable bed for a good night's sleep after all the excitement of the past few days.

Early next morning, I headed over to the local travel agent's, where I managed to secure the last seat on a flight to Paris that night. Even better, it was in

First Class, which I felt was a fair reward for the trials and tribulations of the past three days. That evening I departed for Paris and connected onwards to London for a two-week holiday, and I was only a few days behind my original schedule!

My return home to London coincided with England playing Ireland in a friendly football match in Dublin. I went to the pub with some of my London colleagues to watch the match, but it was soon abandoned after the English fans began a riot in the stands. Riots in Kinshasa and now riots in Dublin! What on earth was going on?

I decided to head home and took the underground back to Willesden Green in the northwest of the city. It was now after 10 pm, and I was the only person walking on the poorly lit street. I suddenly became aware of someone wearing a hoodie walking along beside me. Having had a few beers earlier, I was a little slow to realise that he was mumbling something to me. The words "Give me your wallet" and the knife he began waving in front of my face quickly brought my mind back to sharp focus. A quick glance behind confirmed my worst fears—there were two more hooded figures walking behind me. I couldn't believe that I was being mugged in London, only yards from my own house! I reached slowly into my jacket pocket and handed over my wallet. The three muggers ran off, and I carried on to the house, trembling from the experience. A call to the police and a cursory trip round the block in a police car led to nothing. For the next few days, I carried a sturdy umbrella in my coat for protection, ready to club anyone who might approach me on the street at night, even if it was to ask for directions!

The irony of it all, I thought, was that I had escaped from Kinshasa amid looting, flying bullets and death, and I was now being mugged in London!

"Wrong place, wrong time: it doesn't matter where you are," became my new mantra in life. Somehow, I couldn't help thinking, the sooner I got back to the safety of Kinshasa, the better!

Chapter 6

Many Rivers to Cross

Having survived the Second Pillage in Kinshasa and a mugging in London in the span of a week, the rest of my holiday was rather uneventful. It was now time for me to start thinking about heading back to Zaïre. The situation had settled down, and a sort of uneasy peace had returned to Kinshasa.

I was ready to step back into the wonderful madness of that country again; in fact, I found that I even missed it. After so many months away, London now seemed rather tame—nothing much had changed since I had left. I enjoyed catching up with many friends at my old rugby club, Hampstead RFC, where I had been the first team captain before I moved to Africa, but I realised that people just couldn't relate to the dynamic environment that I was now living in. The conversation would soon get back to topics more familiar for them.

I regularly kept in touch with my London office for news of Kinshasa, and on my last visit to the office, I was asked to bring a microwave back to Kinshasa for one of my colleagues.

At Heathrow, I checked in the microwave with my suitcase. After the recent events in Kinshasa, airlines were no longer flying directly to Kinshasa, with all flights now terminating across the river in Brazzaville. I had experienced this previously in 1992, when airlines had pulled out of Kinshasa for a while due to problems with contaminated jet fuel. At that time, we would disembark in Brazzaville, board an old DC3 and be flown across the river. As business class passengers we had priority, and so we were always flown across first. As someone who loves everything about flying, it was an exhilarating experience taking that DC3, with passengers and luggage packed together inside the cabin. We sat in rickety old seats—some even had seat belts—with rain dripping through holes in the fuselage. The pilots would fire up the propellers, taxi on to the runway, and off we would go, on a wing and a prayer! Fifteen minutes later, we would land on the other side of the river in Kinshasa. Who could ever forget the sight of the pilot wiping the outside of the cockpit window clean for a clear vision as we hurtled down the runway!

With the Second Pillage still fresh in people's minds, the DC3 was unfortunately no longer flying between the two cities. The new plan therefore was for me to be met on arrival in Brazzaville by the local representative for Chevron, the US oil company. I was told that this lady had arranged for me to be taken across the river in the Chevron company speedboat. How exciting!

After an uneventful overnight flight from Brussels, we landed early that Monday morning in Brazzaville. I was met by the Chevron representative and led to a waiting room in the main terminal building. My suitcase and the microwave were brought to the room from the baggage carousel. The room was full of oil workers, either in transit to Pointe-Noire on the coast or heading across to Kinshasa.

I found a seat at the back of the waiting room and sat waiting for my name to be called. Over the next hour, the waiting room steadily grew emptier as groups of people were called out, until I was the last person left in the room. Sitting there, with only my suitcase and microwave as company, I began to wonder whether the arrangements were perhaps not going as smoothly as planned.

My fears were confirmed when the Chevron lady popped her head into the room one last time. Seeing me still sitting there, she asked me what I was still doing in the room. Did I not hear her calling out the Kinshasa departure earlier? I could only put it down to tiredness on my part and confusion over those leaving the room for Pointe Noire and, it now transpired, those leaving for Kinshasa. She gave me a flat look, plainly thinking that I was an imbecile, and informed me that the speedboat had already left for Kinshasa. There was no other means of crossing the river than to go to the port and take a ferry across the river.

There was nothing else she could do, but at least she arranged a driver to take me, my suitcase and the microwave, to the port, wishing me bon chance as I headed off. She said she would call Simon N'Koy in Kinshasa to let him know that I was now going to be taking a ferry across the river sometime that morning.

Arriving at the entrance to the port, I needed to buy a ticket for the ferry crossing, and looked to see what cash I had. Unusually for me, I only had a USD20 bill and some British pounds in my wallet. The pounds were useless in Brazzaville. I had no idea what a ticket cost but knew that I would need to pay for it in CFA Francs. There were several money changers hanging around the entrance, so I headed over, and after a spot of haggling, changed my few dollars for 10,000 CFA Francs.

I headed over to the ticket office, only to be told that a ticket cost CFA 15,000. I was short CFA 5,000. Looking around, I spotted an elderly European couple walking towards the exit, and ran over to them. Putting on my saddest looking face, I introduced myself and explained the predicament that I was in, having missed my transport across the river.

"Would it be possible," I asked, "to borrow CFA 5,000 so I could get back across the river?"

I explained that I worked at an international bank in Kinshasa and would be happy to arrange for the money to be sent to them once I was back in the city. The couple were Swedish missionaries working in Brazzaville; however, by the sceptical look on the face of the husband, I didn't get the feeling I was going to receive much Christian charity from him that day. Thankfully, his wife took pity on my situation and persuaded her husband to hand over the cash. With much thanks and shaking of hands, I returned to the ticket office and bought my ticket. With a great sense of relief, I sat dockside with my luggage to wait for the next sailing across the great river. One is never left alone for long in Africa, however, and I was soon approached by a man in uniform. He asked to see my vaccination card. Flicking through its yellow pages, he informed me that my cholera vaccination had expired. To cross to Kinshasa, I would need to take the vaccine at the port!

This being the era of rampant AIDS, there was no way I was going to expose myself to a potentially unhygienic needle. In fact, part of the survival kit provided by the Head Office included sterile syringes for that very purpose; however, I did not carry them when I travelled. I explained to the official that a cholera vaccination was no longer a requirement for Zaïre, but I was happy to have it updated once I was back in the city. He was quite insistent on the issue, so I finally gave up and paid a "fine" with the remaining pounds in my wallet. I was now totally broke!

I was then confronted with the next problem. A customs official approached and asked me what I was carrying in the box. In French, a microwave is called a micro-onde, and in this part of the world where suspicion of foreigners ran high, I thought the word could be misconstrued. I really didn't want to explain what a micro-onde was, so I told him it was a stereo turntable for playing records. After all, it had a plate which spun, so it was a plausible idea, at least to my mind. To my surprise, he appeared to accept this and walked away.

People were now beginning to gather their belongings and move towards the ferry to board. Many of them were market traders plying their trade between the two cities and had lots of bulky packages and bags to be loaded on board by porters. I began to be pestered by the porters to carry my belongings onto the ferry for a fee. I had to patiently explain that I really had no money whatsoever, an excuse they no doubt had heard from many a mondelé over the years. They still insisted on carrying my suitcase and the microwave on board. To their obvious disgust, instead of handing over any money, I proceeded to hand out packets of my duty-free Marlboro's. At least they had the good grace to accept them and leave, rather than grab my stuff and unload it off the boat, or worse, throw it (and me) overboard!

I settled on a bench on the lower deck until we finally pushed away and headed out into the river. I was now a hundred Marlboro lighter, but still had my possessions, and was on my way home. I just hoped that the message had got through to Simon on the other side that I was coming over on the ferry.

Half an hour later, we were pulling up alongside the dock in Kinshasa, the same dock from where I had departed in vastly different circumstances some weeks before. Amongst the scrum of people alongside, I spotted Simon with his trademark grin, no doubt enjoying the fact that I had been forced to experience a part of life not normally experienced by us expatriates. I hoped that perhaps he might also have felt a little proud of me for getting myself back to Kinshasa without his usual helping hand to smooth the way.

Just another experience of Africa, I thought as I was driven back to my apartment, but it felt good to be home. The micro-onde was safely delivered to its final resting place, no worse for wear from the experience. If only it knew what I had gone through to get it there! Sadly, I never did come across my Swedish saviours again, and still owe them CFA 5,000. Oh, and I never did get that cholera injection in Kinshasa after all!

Chapter 7

A Mélange of Memories

For many years, long before I had arrived in Kinshasa, there were suspicions that something was not quite right in the bank. It was always suspected that some form of fraud had been, and continued to be, perpetrated. Bank records had been lost or were missing. Invariably, at some point, the Head Office would draw a line under the whole sorry mess; losses would be written off, and the whole process would start again.

One of my first roles after I arrived was to try and re-create an audit trail from a jigsaw puzzle of incomplete bank statements and papers we had on the table in front of us. Our task was to see if we could find where the money had gone. It was a thankless task and led us up many a cul-de-sac.

And then, in 1993, the fraud—or at least one of the frauds—was discovered by accident. One of the junior employees in the Trade Finance Department attempted to authorise a large US dollar payment to another local bank in Kinshasa using an Export License as justification for the payment. When the supporting documentation was checked, it was found that the Export License had previously been used on another legitimate transaction, and he was caught out. Having been caught red handed in the act, he proceeded to name some, but not all, of his co-conspirators in the bank. It was clear that there were others he was not prepared to name, perhaps fearful for his own long-term well-being.

I could understand his reticence when the scale of the fraud became clearer—involving several of the senior Heads of Department within the bank acting in concert with unknown accomplices in the Central Bank, the Banque du Zaïre, another local commercial bank, and certain members of the military.

The attempted fraud was discovered a couple of days before I was due to fly back to the UK on my next home leave. Once again, fate had thrown a curve ball at me days before I was due to leave the country. After doing as much as I could to help my expatriate colleagues in handling the situation, it was agreed that I should head home as originally planned, as the situation appeared to be under control.

I set off early that Friday morning for the Swissair flight to Geneva. I was joined in the VIP lounge at the airport by my good friends Greg and Lynda, heading back to Canada for a well-earned break. I was looking forward to sharing a glass or two of wine with them on the flight back to Europe.

As we sat in the lounge, the aircraft was noticeably absent. Usually, it would have arrived the night before from Geneva and be ready for the next leg back via Libreville, Gabon, the next morning. The inbound flight was obviously running late, but we weren't unduly concerned.

The time of our scheduled departure came and went, and there was still no sign of the aircraft. After another hour passed, Swissair finally announced that the aircraft was grounded in Libreville because of a technical fault. A replacement part would have to be flown out from Geneva, and the aircraft was now expected to arrive the following morning. We were advised to head home and return the following morning for the rescheduled departure.

I got a lift back with Greg and Lynda into the city and rang John, the Head of the Bank, to tell him that I would be staying in Kinshasa for another day and would therefore come to the office.

To my surprise, John advised me not to get anywhere close to the bank. It had been raided that morning by a team of officials from the Central Bank. They had informed him that they were taking over full management control, citing the recently discovered fraud as evidence of the poor management of the bank by the expatriate team.

John said that he and my colleague, Peter, had been escorted from the premises and prevented from entering the building. He also said that the head of the delegation had asked about my whereabouts. He had informed them that I had left the country that morning on holiday and had assumed I was now long clear of Zaïrean airspace! He recommended that perhaps it would be best for me to lay low at Greg and Lynda's overnight and get the flight out in the morning as planned. Under no circumstances was I to go near the bank or our residences.

I spent the rest of the day and night at Greg and Lynda's mulling over this new development, half expecting a knock on the door at any moment as the hours slowly passed. Thankfully, the night passed without incident, and we were up early the next morning and heading back to the airport. As we were shown into the VIP lounge for the second time, I was relieved to see the aircraft out on the apron. I sat fidgeting nervously in the lounge, watching the hands on the clock on the wall inch ever so slowly towards boarding time. Every time the lounge door opened and a soldier came in clutching a radio in one hand and papers in the other, my heart dropped as I half expected a hand to be placed on my shoulder to lead me away for questioning.

There was one last hurdle to negotiate, the walk out to the aircraft. There were always military and other officials standing around on the tarmac, any one of whom could stop you and ask to see your documents or contents of your hand luggage. In my current nervous state, I was thankful to be ignored and gratefully boarded the flight. As the aircraft's wheels left the runway, I was finally able to relax and enjoy a refreshing gin and tonic.

Two weeks later, I was on my way back to Kinshasa. Nothing much had changed whilst I was away; the bank was still under the control of the Central

Bank team. During my absence, John and Peter had managed to inform our overseas correspondents not to accept any instructions received from the bank and had closed all foreign currency payment transactions to ensure that no unauthorised payments could be made. They had moved operations to the South African embassy in Kinshasa and had been operating out of the embassy ever since.

As a South African owned bank, the takeover was seen as an attack on South African interests in the country. The appropriate message expressing the potential repercussions of the action had been passed up through Government channels by the South African Ambassador. In the meantime, Simon, N'Koy, had utilised his own contacts with the Government to try and find a resolution to the situation.

Within days of my return, Simon had arranged a lunch meeting with a man who had strong connections to President Mobutu. The lunch would be held at John's house, and I was asked to join. Our guest, we were told, was President Mobuto's enforcer in Kinshasa, a man apparently known as 'The Terminator'. I understood that this was not because he happened to like that film, but was due to his reputation in terminating, shall we say, awkward problems!

The Terminator arrived at John's house on the duly appointed day. He was a small, politely spoken man, immaculately dressed in an expensive suit. He certainly didn't appear to justify his fearsome reputation, but I wasn't going to test it out. Over a splendid lunch, John, in his calm Scottish manner, set out the background to the difficult situation that we faced at the bank. At the end of the discussion, The Terminator informed us that the takeover of the bank had been the work of the "Clique du Kivu", a faction within the Government power structure with its roots in the east of the country. His advice was that we should prepare a one-page memorandum for him, setting out the facts of the situation, and he would deliver it personally to President Mobutu for further action.

A few days later, the memorandum was delivered to The Terminator. Within a couple of days, we were suddenly informed that the bank was to be handed back, and we were invited to the building for a formal handover ceremony. After speeches and smiles all round, we took possession of the building again. It would seem that the "Clique du Kivu" had been sent some sort of "message" from on high. Clearly, the intervention of The Terminator had had the desired effect! Perhaps the man's reputation was justified after all! We never had cause to call upon his services again after that.

During my time in Kinshasa, I had heard rumours that there was an Irish priest working in the city, but I had never come across him. One weekend I was playing golf with the South Korean military attaché in a tournament, and as we chatted, he asked me if I knew the Irish priest. Upon hearing that I had not, he insisted that I come to dinner the following week to meet him. The military attaché was Catholic and regularly attended his Sunday mass.

That Saturday evening, I duly arrived at the

military attaché's house, removed my shoes as is the custom, and entered. The Irish priest arrived soon after, and I was pleasantly surprised to see that he was about my age and dressed casually in a pair of jeans and a shirt. Even better, he said that he would have a beer and lit up a cigarette. I like this guy already, I thought. He was great company, full of amusing stories and anecdotes. As we chatted, I noticed that the table was set for five people and wondered who the fifth guest would be. The mystery was solved half an hour later, and I was introduced to the new Papal Nuncio in Kinshasa. He was Vietnamese, and arrived dressed in the full regalia befitting someone of his position in the Church as the Pope's ambassador. He was a rather serious man, not given to small talk, and quite the opposite of the Irish priest. He asked for an orange juice. The South Korean attaché's wife called us to the table for dinner, and we took our places. She had prepared a wide range of dishes, all exquisitely presented. It was the first time that I was introduced to Kimchi, the traditional Korean dish of fermented spiced vegetables, often cabbage-based. Kimchi is traditionally prepared and then buried in clay pots for a lengthy period, until it has developed an incredibly strong and fiery flavour. After our first taste, the priest and I were gasping and reaching for our beers to douse the fire in our mouths, much to the amusement of our hosts.

I was in the middle of a rather amusing tale with the priest when, out of the corner of my eye, I noticed the Papal Nuncio handing a set of rosary beads, and what turned out to be medals of the Virgin Mary, to our host's wife. She very deferentially requested him to bless them. Before we knew what was happening, they had put down their cutlery and launched into a full round of the Stations of the Cross, blessing each medal along the way!

Rather sheepishly, my new friend and I joined in, mumbling our way through the remaining Our Fathers and Hail Mary's—in my case, words vaguely remembered—until we finally reached the conclusion of the proceedings. Our conversation resumed where we had left off, whilst our hosts continued to discuss matters of the church with the Papal Nuncio. Much to our relief, there were no further religious icons proffered, and we continued to enjoy our Korean hospitality until it was time to head home.

Sadly, for whatever reason, I never did meet up with that Irish priest again in Kinshasa, and cannot even remember his name. I only hope he wasn't exiled to the bush by the austere Papal Nuncio as a penance for his rather less than pious lifestyle in Kinshasa!

John, my boss, was heading back to the UK for Christmas, leaving Peter and myself holding the fort in Kinshasa. On the flight, he found himself sitting beside an elegant, well-dressed Congolese woman in business class. They struck up a polite conversation, and it became clear to him that she was aware of who he was, although perhaps it was not that surprising given the fact that he was the Country Head of a large international bank. She appeared to also know about myself and Peter. John realised that she must be well connected to the President and powers that be in Kinshasa, given her detailed knowledge of the expatriates living there. There was no doubt that we were being watched; indeed, in hindsight, I now understand why there were always a couple of men standing beside a conveniently broken-down taxi outside the gates of the apartment complex where I lived.

As their conversation continued over canapés and champagne, she wondered whether the Bank might be able to help with some Government business. She wanted the bank to open a Letter of Credit to cover the importation of frozen chicken from the UK. It seemed that the President wanted them to feed the military that Christmas. She told John that if he agreed, ninety thousand dollars in cash would be brought to the Bank in Kinshasa to cover the cost of the chickens.

John couldn't really refuse, and so, on arriving in the UK, he contacted us and advised us to open the Letter of Credit once the funds had been brought to the bank. A few days later, the cash was deposited, and the Letter of Credit issued.

A week later, a refrigerated lorry containing the frozen chickens arrived at Gatwick Airport, to be loaded onto a cargo flight to Kinshasa. The ground crew realised, however, that with all the other freight on board, there was not enough room in the hold for all the palettes of chicken. One pallet would have to be left behind. As a result, that evening, a local radio station sent out an appeal to homeless charities in the Gatwick area to come and collect free frozen chickens from the airport.

And so it came to pass, that His Excellency Mobutu Sese Seko, President of Zaïre, fed the homeless of South London on Christmas Day!

My wife, Fiona, came to Kinshasa twice during my time there. The first, in August 1993, was at the tail end of our honeymoon which we had spent in Zimbabwe.

On her second short visit the following year, Fiona arrived without incident and spent a week exploring the delights of the city, having been taken under the wing of an old hand, Lynda. At the end of the week, I took her back to the airport for the evening flight back to Brussels. Simon N'Koy was on holiday, so it was left to me to navigate the airport bureaucracy on my own. The first problem that we encountered when we arrived was that the VIP lounge was closed. We had no option but to head to the main terminal building to check in.

We entered the hot and humid terminal to be confronted with chaotic scenes: people shouting, pushing, and shoving, masses of bags everywhere. There was but one thing to be done—to stride purposely forward, pushing aside anyone ahead of us until we were able to get to the business class check-in desk.

This was the first time that I had used the main airport terminal in the almost two years of working in Kinshasa. I needed to keep Fiona close to me to ensure she got through the chaos, particularly as she did not speak or understand French. Finally, with her boarding pass in hand, we headed to the security check. One of the female security officers took particular interest in Fiona and specifically in any items of value she might have on her. She insisted on taking Fiona into a side room for a pat down and perhaps a petit cadeau, a small gift. I waited nervously for a few minutes until she reappeared, looking quite relaxed and none the worse for the experience. The fact she understood no French was probably a benefit.

Her flight was being called for boarding, so we headed for the gate. We walked through the departure gate, and I pointed out the SABENA 747 some way off to the right of us. There were several other aircraft on the apron between us and the 747, and I wanted to make sure Fiona knew which aircraft to head for. A hurried goodbye kiss and she walked away.

As she disappeared behind the aircraft, I was confronted by a security official wanting to know what I was doing on the aircraft side of the terminal. He went to grab my arm, so I quickly turned and headed back into the terminal and out to my waiting car. The last thing I needed was to be arrested, especially on a Friday night!

We were about halfway back when I realised that I had never actually seen Fiona board the aircraft! Given the amount of security personnel standing around on the tarmac she could have been stopped and prevented from boarding at any time and I would have been none the wiser, particularly as we had no means of communication. There followed a sleepless night until I called Fiona the next morning and was pleased to hear she had arrived safely back home in London!

One of the joys of living in Kinshasa was to be able to get away from the city over the weekend for a few hours and enjoy some down time with friends. That could be a day spent on the river, or at an old holiday camp a few hours' drive from Kinshasa, called Black River. One of the places I hadn't been to before was a beach located west of the city on the banks of the Zaïre River, close to the famous rapids. A group of us decided that it would be fun to spend a Sunday at the beach.

The Bank had just purchased a new red Land Rover Discovery, which was the pride and joy of my colleague, Peter, our operations manager. He happened to be out of the country on holiday, so my new South African colleague Colin and I were holding the fort. We felt that it would be an ideal opportunity to try out the Discovery's off-road qualities.

We set off that morning in a convoy of 4x4s. After about five miles, we turned off the main road and followed a rough track through the bush for some time until we arrived at the riverbank and beach. There was a steep incline down to the main beach area, which we slowly descended one by one, and parked. At this point, we noticed that we were missing a metal grill over one of the rear lights on the new car, which must have come off during the drive.

We spent the day enjoying cold beer and food. At one point, a game of American football started, which got a little feisty and rough at times. Thankfully, by the end of the day, there were no broken bones to take back to the city. By 4 pm, it was time to pack up and head back before dark. As I had driven out that morning, Colin would drive us back.

Colin and I were in the last car of the convoy

following our Canadian friend Greg. Colin struggled to keep up with Greg on the unfamiliar bush track. As the sun began to set, our only reference point for the road ahead became the rear lights ahead of us. We came upon a sudden sharp left-hand turn at speed, and in trying to follow the bend felt the Discovery slide in the soft sand and come to a sudden stop with a bang. Colin revved the engine to try and pull us forward, but to no avail. We appeared to be well and truly stuck. We got out and saw that the back of the Discovery had slid off the track into deep soft sand and was wedged against a small tree trunk. We began to clear the sand away from around the rear tires to try and free ourselves as night fell. Despite our increasingly desperate attempts, we were unable to force the car to budge.

Just as we were beginning to think that we might be stuck for the night, we saw lights approaching. Greg had turned back once he realised that we were no longer behind him. It was clear that we would need to pull out the Discovery using his 4x4. Luckily, he had a rope in his car, which he had only thrown into the boot that morning. He must have had a premonition! Colin tied the rope to our front bumper and Greg proceeded to pull our car slowly out of the sand. Two things then happened; the rope snapped just at the very moment our car came free, and a loud screech of wrenching metal came from the rear. In the dark, we hadn't noticed that the rear bumper had been wedged behind the tree trunk and was ripped off as it was pulled free.

Relieved that we were free, we continued home without further incident. Peter was returning to Kinshasa in the coming days, so we needed to get the Discovery repaired as quickly as possible in the hope he wouldn't notice the damage done. The local Land Rover dealer could repair the rear bumper, but would need to order a replacement metal grill for the rear light from Europe. It would not arrive before Peter's return.

The next day, I happened to mention the missing metal grill to one of our companions that day on the beach. To my surprise, he told me that he had the metal grill! On the drive back from the beach, he had been stopped by a boy on the track waving the grill. The boy had found it and waited for the cars to return and sold it back to my friend.

What a stroke of luck! We were delighted to be able to hand the repaired Discovery back to Peter on his return, none the wiser to its traumatic experience in the bush!

Chapter 8

The Last Supper

After two of the most exciting years of my life, living and working in Kinshasa, the time had come to return to the UK. It was June 1994, and I was saddened to be leaving this great city and country and the people that I had grown to love.

My replacement, Marc, had arrived from South Africa a few weeks earlier, and still looked a little uneasy in his new environment. His anxiety had not been helped by his arrival in Kinshasa without a proper visa which, thankfully, Simon N'Koy had been able to smooth over at the airport. Already in a state of nervous tension, his peace of mind wasn't helped when we took him for lunch on the day he arrived.

His first meal in Kinshasa turned out to be a plate of raw mince with an egg yolk on top. His face went rather pale as the dish was placed in front of him. Kinshasa had some of the best restaurants I had ever eaten in, so I had no concerns about his choice, but in his mind, eating raw meat on his first day was probably a step too far! It turned out when ordering, he had thought that the 'steak americain' was a hamburger, when in fact he had ordered the Belgian version of a steak tartar! Not a great start to his new life in Kinshasa for the next few years.

He showed little enthusiasm to get to know the city in those first few weeks, and, no doubt fearing for his safety, ended up spending most of his time when not in the office locked in his house with only his cigarettes, beer, and videos for company.

Meanwhile, a farewell lunch had been arranged for the 10th of June with twelve of my closest friends in the wine cellar, the "cave", of the Intercontinental Hotel. I was looking forward to a long relaxing Friday, with good food and wine in great company. The day would end later that evening at the British Embassy, where we would be celebrating the Queen's birthday.

That morning I was working in my office when Simon N'Koy popped his head in. He told me that there was a military officer in his office with a warrant for my arrest. Well, you don't get that kind of news every day, but being in Zaïre, where anything is possible, it didn't come as an enormous surprise. I asked Simon to show the officer into my office. He was a tall, well-built man, wearing a maroon beret and camouflage fatigues, a pistol in a holster on his hip. I examined the document bearing several official stamps with my name clearly written on it. It appeared that I was to be taken to the SARM military intelligence headquarters for questioning. On what grounds, I was not sure.

Simon advised that it was best for me to go with the officer, and he would follow behind and see if he could sort out the problem there. I grabbed my satellite phone, and on the way out, casually informed Marc that I was being arrested. I wasn't sure how long I would be away, but he was in charge until I got back.

I got into the soldier's car and we headed off up the Boulevard du 30 Juin, followed by Simon in his own car. Fifteen minutes later, we turned in to a military compound and parked outside an office building. I was put in a room and left sitting on my own. Simon disappeared into the building to find out what was going on.

As I was alone, I quickly turned on my satellite phone. At that moment it rang and Sam, the private security contractor we had sought refuge with during the Second Pillage, called to let me know that he would be coming to my lunch.

"Ah," I said, "slight problem in that I am not sure I can make my lunch. I have been arrested and am currently sitting in military intelligence headquarters."

Sam's job provided him with many contacts within the Zaïrean military apparatus, and he offered to make some calls. I asked him not to, as I didn't want to complicate matters further until I knew what the exact situation was.

Simon popped back in to tell me that he had been told to leave the barracks. He said that he would try to contact a prominent expatriate businessman we knew well, as he had some influence with the authorities. I figured that if anyone could get me out, he could, but until I knew what was going on, the only course of action was to remain calm and see how things developed.

A little later, my arresting officer returned and led me down a corridor to another office. On entering, I saw three men dressed in civilian clothes sitting behind a table. I was told to sit on the chair facing them. After looking at their notes, they proceeded to ask me several questions.

"How long have you been in Zaïre?"

"Two years".

"Where have you been working in Kinshasa?"

"At the South African bank"

"Who do you know in Kinshasa?"

Well, this last question made me pause for thought. If I started mentioning specific names, could I potentially be putting them in a difficult situation? On the other hand, if I said that I knew no one, they would obviously call this out as a lie—it was surely unbelievable that I should know no one in the city after two years. I figured that the best response would be to say that I knew some people in the Zaïrean military, such as the DSP and indeed SARM itself, from playing rugby. By implying that I was friendly with and knew various military personnel in those units, it might make it a little easier on me from hereon.

"Which expatriates do you know in Kinshasa?"

Again, I felt that the best response would be to name one of the best-known expatriates in town, the same guy Simon was going to call for assistance. He ran a very successful and popular milk powder business in Kinshasa. At the mention of his name, they wrote his name down and underlined it twice.

Oops, I thought, I hope I haven't dragged you into this mess now as well!

I felt confident enough to ask them why I was being held: what charges were being levelled against me?

One of the men said that I would be told in due course, but that the charges were quite serious. I commented that it would be good to know sooner rather than later, as I was due to leave the country permanently in a week's time.

He said that he thought that might not be possible now, given the situation.

"Ah," I replied, "Then I guess I had better call my wife in London and let her know I might be a little late coming home!"

With that, the meeting came to an end, and I was escorted back to the other room. As I sat waiting, my expatriate businessman friend arrived. I was delighted to see his friendly face and felt confident that my predicament would be resolved quickly. He went off to talk to my interrogators and returned soon after not looking at all confident.

"Hell, this is serious, Mike."

He had tried to reason with them, he told me, but they were adamant that I was to be held over the weekend! He had, however, managed to negotiate my release for the day; but it had cost him a six-hundred-dollar bond! I was to be returned to the barracks by six o'clock that evening.

I was offered a salute by my arresting officer as I got into the car. Heading back into town, I asked my rescuer whether I should just go home, grab my passport, and make a run for the airport for the evening flight to Brussels.

He had, on several occasions, been through similar situations himself. He advised me that there was no need for such a drastic move. The best thing to do would be to return later, dressed in jeans and a t-shirt, and to bring some cash and cigarettes with me. These would help keep anyone held in the cell with me on my side.

"In the meantime, we have a lunch to get to," he concluded, and we headed off in the direction of the Intercontinental Hotel.

We arrived to find the other guests already waiting in the "cave". Given the morning's events, I felt that a gin and tonic would steady my nerves, but decided to stay off the alcohol over lunch to remain sober for my return to the barracks. I recounted my experience to the assembled group. Two of those present worked at the British and American Embassies and volunteered to make some calls to see if that would help. They hurried out of the room with their satellite phones.

They returned after a while. They had been unable to get any further information.

Lunch was ready, and we were called to our seats at a long table surrounded by bottles of wine in their racks. As I filled my water glass, my rescuer stood up to offer a farewell toast in my honour. Raising our glasses, he went on to tell me that he had been impressed with how I had handled myself that morning in very difficult circumstances.

He then announced that my arrest, interrogation,

and incarceration had been a set-up organised by him and some of the assembled group as my final parting gift from Zaïre!

He hoped that I had enjoyed the experience as one which I would remember for a very long time. The good news was that I would no longer be required back at the barracks that evening!

I don't think I have ever laughed as much as I did at that moment, enjoying both the relief at being spared a weekend in the military barracks and the sheer audacity of organising a stunt like that. Given the tense situation in the country, there were so many things that could have gone wrong, with all manner of repercussions for me.

I was later told that it had taken the military guys some time to understand that the arrest was to be just a joke, "une comédie anglaise," I believe they called it. These guys arrested people for real, so there was always the possibility that someone higher up the chain of command might turn it into a real life situation. I also found out much later that certain partners of the conspirators were unhappy about it, given the serious risks involved. However, the pranksters had always banked on the fact that I would remain calm throughout and not react in a way that made matters worse for myself. Given my generally laid back and cheerful outlook on life, they were confident that I would be alright. Thankfully, I had played my part exactly as they had hoped.

Released from the prospect of a weekend in the barracks, I swiftly made up for my lack of alcohol consumption and proceeded to catch up with the others. An extremely enjoyable long lunch carried on into the early evening, by which time it was time to decamp to the British Embassy for the evening reception in honour of the Queen.

We carried on at the Embassy bar late into the evening, by which time I was feeling the effects of my long day. My last, rather hazy, memory of the night, before being taken home, is of hanging off the shoulder of the Chilean military attaché, proclaiming loudly, "You'll never believe what happened to me today!" and recounting my story!

I was pleased to wake up in my own bed rather than a cell the next morning, albeit a little worse for wear. I thought that I had better check in with my new South African colleague, whom I hadn't heard from since I had been "arrested" the previous day. From what I heard later, the moment I was taken away from the bank, he had packed up his desk in a panic, and had gone straight back to his house, locked himself in, and stayed there for the rest of the weekend!

And so, at dawn on Friday, 17 June 1994, two years after first setting foot in Kinshasa, I closed the door to my apartment for the final time. I headed downstairs to the waiting car for the long drive out to the airport. The drive itself was uneventful until we turned into the airport terminal approach road and two Guarde Civile stepped out into the road and waved at us to pull over.

In my two years in Zaïre, I had never seen the airport security move from their posts, let alone order a vehicle to stop. With my "arrest" the week before still fresh in my mind, I smelt a rat and the hand of the practical jokers playing one last hand. I casually instructed my driver to ignore them.

To my surprise, they stood their ground, and instead raised their rifles menacingly.

I couldn't believe it. After two years of coming and going through the airport without a hindrance, I was being stopped on my final day—and we could have been shot in the process in my mistaken belief that this was one final leaving present from the gang! Naturally, we pulled over, had our papers checked, and were finally waved on towards the terminal and that welcoming VIP lounge for a final time.

As the wheels of the Swissair MD-11 lifted off the runway and we turned north towards Europe, my thoughts dwelt on my time spent in Zaïre and the good friends I had made there. I had loved every minute and wouldn't have swapped my experiences, good and bad, for any money. Zaïre would always remain a part of me, exemplified by the spirit of the people who, despite the crippling poverty, hardships, and brutality they faced daily, were still able to laugh and enjoy life as best they could. My time in Zaïre was perhaps best summarised in the words of the famous Congolese singer Koffi Olomide "Cą c'est bon cą!"

PART II

New Frontiers to Explore

Chapter 9

The Wild Geese

In 2001, I moved to a Belgian bank in London and was running the Africa desk. I would often get enquiries related to potential business opportunities in various parts of Africa. My favourite was the Belgian chap who rang and asked about the possibility of doing business with him in Rwanda and Burundi. I explained that these countries didn't form part of our strategic focus in Africa. He was surprised, given that both were former Belgian colonies and with us being a Belgian bank, why not? I asked him how many countries he knew in Africa that spoke Flemish.

Perplexed, he replied—none. I explained that we were in fact a Flemish Belgian bank. If he wanted to do business in French speaking Africa, he might be better off going to a French Belgian bank!

Having said that, I had the unique experience of being one of the first London-based bankers to undertake a business trip to Equatorial Guinea. Not a country on the usual list of places to visit, but we had received a promising enquiry to support the country's growing offshore oil production, which was worth investigating further.

I didn't really know too much about the country other than it was composed of two parts, the mainland with its capital, Bata, and an offshore island, Bioko, with its capital Malabo. Being a former Spanish colony, Spanish was the spoken language, although French was rapidly taking over as the lingua franca of the day.

The country was headed by President Teodoro Obiang Nguema, who had overthrown his paranoid dictator uncle in a coup in 1979 and seized power for himself. He was one of Africa's longest serving rulers. Significant oil reserves had been discovered off Bioko, making it an important new player in the global crude oil market and a new strategic partner for the US.

After several meetings in London, a date was finally set for our first visit to this mysterious country. My colleague David and I duly set off from London flying via Madrid, where we were joined by a colleague from our Madrid office. We boarded the flight to Malabo at two in the morning, along with the many expatriate oil workers returning to work on the offshore oil platforms and the giant methane gas plant located on the island.

Four hours later, we finally began our descent into Malabo. In a scene reminiscent of my time spent in Zaïre, the airport tarmac was busy with armed soldiers milling about, sporting the ubiquitous designer sunglasses, and looking as menacing as possible. We disembarked and were met by a waiting delegation.

We were led to a VIP cabin where we completed our immigration and baggage formalities. This was so very like Kinshasa that I almost felt that I had landed in the wrong country!

Formalities completed, we left the airport in a convoy of 4x4's and were driven through the sleepy city streets. We arrived at the gates of a large newly built complex comprising a conference centre recently used to host an Africa Union Heads of State meeting and luxury villas. We were dropped at one of the villa's and settled in.

After freshening up, we were joined by those we had met in London for discussions prior to our meeting with the Government ministers planned for later that day. Our hosts were an interesting mix, a young well-spoken Lebanese man, who had previously worked at Credit Suisse, a former presidential adviser to Pascal Lissouba, the former President of the Republic of Congo, and the wife of the former President of Guinea!

We spent most of the day working on a presentation in Spanish which we would present to the ministers later. It was clear however that there was no formal timetable or schedule in place, and we would be summoned to meetings as and when it was convenient for the Government. After a long tiring day, we finally received a call at 6.30 pm to go to an address in the city.

We were driven to a nondescript building which we took to be a school. On the second floor we were shown into a room, with two long tables facing each other. Sitting on the one side were eight Government representatives. We were introduced to the Minister of Labour and the Minister of Economy and their colleagues. We took our places on the opposite side and the meeting commenced. It became obvious from an early stage that the Government delegation appeared to be split into two camps, one faction led by the Minister of Labour and the other by the Minister of Economy. Each would disrupt and contradict the other's position. The conclusion we came to was that each was vying to position itself in favour with the President and if this meant taking an opposite position to the other faction then this is what they did. This led to a somewhat chaotic meeting in which any apparent progress made with one side would be contradicted with an opposite view from the other faction and we would start the whole process again.

The discussions carried on late into the night. At one point, my colleague David was in the middle of a lengthy and detailed explanation of the type of information we would need from the Government to support any financing when I took it upon myself to rearrange some loose papers lying untidily on the desk. As I collected the papers together, I watched in horror as David's brand new PalmPilot slid out and crashed to the floor, shattering into pieces. I had not seen it nestling amongst the papers.

I was impressed with David's ability to carry on, seemingly unperturbed whilst I scrambled around under the table, trying to recover the pieces of his expensive new toy in the vain hope that it could be reassembled. I could only mutter heartfelt apologies and offer to replace it in due course!

The meeting was concluded with some rather vague assurances that we would be provided with the relevant oil information at some later point.

The next day we were about to head out to look around the city when we received a telephone call summoning us to the Presidential Palace for a meeting with President Obiang himself. This was unexpected and we quickly suited up and headed off to the Palace. When we arrived, we were shown to a waiting room by his Moroccan security team and told that only two of our party would be allowed to meet the President. David and I were the obvious candidates, so we were led into a separate room and relieved of pens, watches, jewellery, and any other items the security team deemed a threat to the President's life. We were then brought into a large ornate furnished room, instructed to sit on two chairs and await the entrance of His Excellency.

The President entered from a side door and sat on what looked like a throne opposite us. It was rather unsettling to be sitting in front of a man with a reputation for allegedly eating the testicles of his enemies, and I felt as if my own were retracting into my own body just in case! We spent about thirty minutes with the President, providing him with a short introduction about ourselves, our company, and the purpose of our visit. At the end of our half hour, we were dismissed and returned to collect our belongings, relieved to leave the Palace with all our body parts intact.

We accomplished little beyond our first meeting

with the ministers and the President and were requested to return to Malabo a few weeks later when we would be provided with the additional information we had sought. This would then allow us to make a proper assessment of a financing proposal for further negotiation with the Government.

A month later I received the call from our contacts to return to Malabo. I was instructed to fly to Libreville, Gabon where we would meet up with a government delegation from Equatorial Guinea attending a meeting in Libreville and fly back to Malabo with them.

My colleague from Madrid joined me in Paris for the flight to Libreville. We landed early the following morning and made our way to the business transit lounge to await the arrival of the delegation from Equatorial Guinea. After several hours there was still no sign of them. We dozed on and off throughout the morning until around noon when a Russian made AN32 aircraft bearing the Equatorial Guinea flag on its tail landed and taxied to the far end of the terminal. We took the aircraft's arrival as a sign that the delegation had concluded its meetings in the city and was on its way to the airport for the return flight to Malabo.

An hour later, the doors to the lounge opened and the delegation entered. They completely ignored us as we stood waiting to make our introductions and instead went straight to the duty-free shop and purchased expensive watches and other luxury items. Once done, a member of the delegation came over and told us that they were heading back into Libreville for lunch so our departure would not be until later in the afternoon.

Having sat in the lounge for over five hours with little to eat or drink, the thought of having lunch was too tempting. However, there was one small problem. We were in transit to Malabo and therefore did not have a visa to enter Gabon. We spoke to the immigration officer in the lounge who assured us that this wasn't a problem, stamped our passports and let us out of the lounge. We jumped into a taxi and headed to the Radisson Blu hotel in the city. We sat for lunch on the outside terrace looking out over the Atlantic Ocean and were pleased to see that the government delegation was also at the hotel, so we could take our time.

Once it looked like the delegation was finishing, my colleague and I headed back to the airport and were readmitted to the lounge. The delegation arrived soon after and proceeded down to the tarmac where delegates from the Gabonese government were waiting to formally send off their counterparts from Malabo. We were told to head straight to the aircraft and wait. We walked up the rear loading ramp into the cabin which was configured in three sections. At the rear was a VIP section, then a central cargo section and finally a forward seating area for passengers. We watched as various people came on board with suitcases, bags, sacks, boxes and even a bicycle and just left them in a pile lying around the cargo section.

Looking at the mess around us, my colleague and I took it upon ourselves to rearrange the cargo into a neat and orderly pile to maximise the storage space. This amused the flight crew greatly who probably weren't used to seeing two foreign "dignitaries" getting their hands dirty loading cargo on an aircraft in the middle of Africa!

Formalities completed, the government delegation boarded, and we took our seats in the forward section. We departed Libreville and flew north towards Bata where we would make a brief stop before continuing our short journey to Malabo. Fifty minutes later we landed in Bata, where everyone disembarked. We sat in the small wooden terminal building drinking soft drinks and began talking to the only member of the delegation who spoke good English. His name was Domingo Mba. A few years later he was appointed head of the state oil company, GEPetrol.

I noticed a large group of people milling around the aircraft and didn't think much of it. The sun was beginning to set when the captain came to tell us it was time to board. The runway had no lights, so we needed to take off before it got dark. We boarded a second time and noticed that the forward seating area was now occupied by the people we had seen earlier. There was nowhere for us to sit so the captain told us to take two of the seats in the VIP section at the back. This resulted in two of the junior members of the delegation giving up their seats to us which they didn't look too pleased about. Soon the plane hurtled down the runway and took off into the dying embers of the sun.

The delegation members in the VIP section ignored us and spent the next thirty minutes talking in high spirits. What they didn't know was that my colleague was Spanish so understood their conversation. It seems they were rather satisfied with themselves believing they had got the better of their Gabonese counterparts in their negotiations!

It was pitch black outside as we descended towards Malabo. We were once again met by our local representatives and driven to a villa in the same complex as before.

We sat for hours the following morning waiting for the information we had been promised. By lunchtime, a car pulled up outside and the driver delivered a bag of croissants and sausage rolls for our lunch. We were a little concerned with the sausage rolls, which appeared to have what looked like shrivelled penises rattling around inside! We wondered perhaps if this was a subtle hint as to what might happen to our manhood if we proved uncooperative! Equatorial Guinea is considered to be the centre of voodoo in West Africa after all!

By the end of the day, no documents had been delivered. We went out for dinner with our hosts and then on to a local nightclub to while away the evening. On Friday morning, someone from the Government arrived at our villa and it was suggested that we should stay in Malabo over the weekend. It appeared that the Government was expecting us to visit each Government Ministry and go through filing cabinets for the information we needed! Clearly that was never going to work. We advised our local contacts that this was a fruitless exercise and decided to cut our losses and catch our scheduled flight to Cameroon that evening and then on to Paris and London. I never heard from our representatives on the ground again after that.

Around three years later the newspapers were filled with stories of the arrest in Zimbabwe of a group of mercenaries led by an ex British SAS soldier and Old Etonian, Simon Mann. The group had left South Africa for Equatorial Guinea and stopped in Zimbabwe to take on board weapons when the plot was exposed. It was alleged that their aim was the overthrow of President Obiang and install a new President in exchange for exclusive oil rights in the country. Following his conviction in Zimbabwe and imprisonment for three years, Mann was secretly extradited to Equatorial Guinea and convicted again in a show trial in Malabo.

It was reported at the time that Zimbabwe's President Mugabe had extradited Mann in exchange for oil supplies which Zimbabwe could not afford to pay for. It was also reported that President Obiang had vowed to sodomise his high-profile prisoner, before skinning him alive and parading his body through Malabo, though thankfully for Mann, this never came to pass, at least the skinning alive and parading of his body through the streets! Who knows, other than Mann himself whether the other occurred behind the walls of Black Beach prison.

I followed the trial in Malabo with great interest. The key plotters were subsequently found guilty and sentenced to long prison terms, Mann receiving thirty-four years, before being surprisingly pardoned by the President in 2009. As I read more details about the alleged coup and its ring leaders, I was stunned to read that the young Lebanese ex-banker, who had been one of the key intermediaries during our meetings with the Government in 2001, had also been convicted of involvement in the coup and had been sentenced to nineteen years imprisonment!

A small world indeed, I thought. I concluded it was probably best not to go back to Equatorial Guinea any time soon just in case I might be deemed guilty by association, arrested, and thrown into the "notorious Black Beach prison," as the newspapers always described it, a place I was certainly not keen to see the inside of!

Having read more about Black Beach since, it seems it fully deserves its appalling reputation.

Chapter 10

The Sting

In 1998, I found myself boarding an Air France flight from Paris to Madagascar with great excitement. I had been given the opportunity to travel to this exotic and little-known country after being asked to take on the account responsibility of a small Paris-based coffee trader. After reviewing the file, I discovered that there were several documents missing relating to coffee that the bank had financed in Madagascar. It was therefore necessary to travel there to check that the coffee was being held in the warehouses on our behalf. I was accompanied on the flight by one of the directors of the company.

After an eleven-hour-long flight, we landed in Antananarivo in the early morning. Collecting our bags, we met up with my client's local agent and were driven to our hotel. My first impression of this fascinating country was that it was very different from mainland Africa. There were paddy fields all around us as we drove into the city, and many of the people appeared to have Asian features. For all intents and purposes, we could have been in Malaysia or Indonesia rather than off the coast of southern Africa.

We spent the day resting, and the following morning we headed back to the airport. We were taking an internal flight to the city of Toamasina, on the east coast. Toamasina, also known as Tamatave, is the principal port of Madagascar, and was a rather interesting city to drive around. I marvelled at the rickshaw taxis plying their trade and the bunches of fresh lychees growing freely in the roadside trees. Freshly picked lychees are delicious, and I picked a bunch to keep in my hotel room for the next morning. We spent the day meeting various companies around the city, but it seemed that no one was in any great hurry to provide my missing paperwork. At the end of the day, we headed back to our hotel to freshen up for dinner.

I was a little underwhelmed by the level of cooperation I was getting so far in my quest for the missing documents, and, whilst they were extremely charming and helpful, I was becoming increasingly suspicious of my companions' motives in continually deflecting questions about the documentation.

We reconvened a little later for dinner in the hotel restaurant. The restaurant was empty apart from our group, and at the end of the meal it was suggested that we move on to a popular nightclub in town to experience some of the local nightlife. I was happy to go, and soon we found ourselves in the club, which was packed with locals and backpackers. We pushed our way to the bar and ordered drinks. My French client was soon chatting to one of the local girls and disappeared onto the dance floor with her. Standing at the bar with my beer, I noticed his local representative talking to a girl and then pointing me out to her.

She quickly appeared at my side and struck up a conversation. I bought her a drink, and we chatted in a mix of broken English and French as I kept a watch on what was happening around me. Eventually, I noticed my French companion leaving the club with the girl. He was followed by his local representative who placed a chair outside the exit to the club and sat down.

What was happening seemed obvious to me by now. I was being set up with a local girl in the hope I would leave with her, and when I did, I would have to pass by the local representative stationed at the door. The question was—how to deal with it? The best course of action would be to leave the club on my own; however, the young lady with me was rather insistent that she come back to my hotel too!

I decided to leave with her and ditch her on the way back to the hotel. Finishing my beer, I walked out with her, bidding goodnight to the sentry posted at the exit and climbed into a waiting rickshaw.

The rickshaw driver started trotting and ten minutes later we were back at the hotel entrance. At this point I informed my companion that this was as far as she was going and peeled off some banknotes to pay her for her time. I had to admire the etiquette of the young lady, who refused to take my money on the basis that no transaction had occurred. She insisted she should come into the hotel with me! I assured her that was not going to happen and in one motion dropped the money in her lap, leapt out of the rickshaw and ran in to the hotel and the safety of my room, feeling rather pleased with myself with having extricated myself from a tricky situation.

Next morning, I woke early, showered, ate some delicious lychees, and headed downstairs for breakfast with a spring in my step. Not to my surprise, my client and his representatives were already sitting at an outside table on the terrace by the hotel entrance having breakfast. The look of disappointment on their faces was a joy to behold as they had clearly expected me to come out with the lady, after having seen me leave the club with her the night before.

Having thwarted their cunning plan, I left Madagascar the next day with the missing paperwork in my possession, and my integrity thankfully still intact!

Chapter 11

An Illegal Immigrant

Sitting in the departure lounge at Entebbe Airport, I figured that it was going to be a while before we departed. It was raining heavily outside with thunder rolling in from Lake Victoria nearby. I was in Uganda for a few days, visiting a major coffee processor and exporter, and we were due to fly to Tanzania to have a look at their operations there. My client had hired a small six-seater plane to fly us south to Mwanza and then on to Bukoba on the western shore of Lake Victoria.

Our two South African pilots had the look of experienced pilots who were used to flying into bush airstrips on some clandestine mission or other. They had informed us that our departure would be delayed until the storms over the Lake had passed. Whilst a commercial airliner could fly through or over them, a small plane like ours could be flung thousands of feet up, or worse, down into the Lake in these storms. So it wasn't safe for us to fly, and we had to wait. I was quite happy to be guided by the pilots and not end up swimming in Lake Victoria with the crocodiles for company!

Three hours later, the rain had subsided, and the storm clouds had passed. We were good to go and boarded the small plane.

We took off and headed south for Mwanza. Although the storms had passed, there remained large threatening cloud formations ahead, which created a significant amount of turbulence, making for a bumpy ride! My companion didn't look so good with all the turbulence and held on tightly to his arm rest throughout the journey.

The flight took about forty minutes, following which we descended into Mwanza to complete immigration formalities with the Tanzanian authorities. With our passports stamped with our entry visas, we set off on the second leg in a northwest direction to Bukoba.

The flight was as bumpy as before, but it wasn't long before we were descending towards Bukoba's airfield. Our pilot told us that we were landing on a dirt runway and with all the rain during the day, there was a chance that the undercarriage might collapse on landing; so we should make sure that we were well strapped in. Well, I loved my job which took me to unusual places, but this was perhaps taking it to extremes. Still, there was no turning back now, so with a silent prayer and a little hint of excitement, we started our approach.

We came in fast and touched down. The undercarriage thankfully held firm, but as we sped down the airstrip, there was a sudden loud bang from the left side of the aircraft. My initial thought was that the undercarriage was gone, but we were still level and slowing down without any apparent damage. We taxied to the small hut that served as the arrivals building and got out. On closer inspection, it turned out that a wing had been hit by a bird on the runway but had sustained no damage.

We were met by the manager of the coffee company, a Cuban. Before we left, the pilots reminded us that we should be back at the airfield for departure no later than 4 pm to return to Mwanza to refuel.

We drove into Bukoba for lunch and then spent the next few hours visiting coffee warehouses and the processing plant. Our Cuban host obviously didn't get many overseas visitors in this far-flung outpost of Tanzania, and was intent on spending as much time as possible with us. He insisted that we go to his house for farewell drinks before our departure. He lived in a large house set on the top of a cliff with commanding views over the lake and Bukoba. It was quite a stunning location. However, 4 pm came and went before we were finally able to bid farewell and head back to the airfield, arriving at 4.30 pm.

Our pilots were annoyed at our late return, and told us to get on board quickly. We took off and flew back to Mwanza in silence as the sun slowly began to set. We landed in Mwanza, where the pilots refuelled the plane and then headed off to immigration with our passports. When they returned, they told us that the immigration officials at the airport had gone home as we had missed them due to our late departure from Bukoba.

An official in the terminal had told the pilots that we could go into Mwanza and stay overnight and get our passports stamped in the morning at the airport. My client decided that there was no way we were staying, as we both had commitments the next day back in Uganda. More so, the pilots informed him that they had now exceeded their flying hours and agreed hire rate, and would need another five hundred dollars. This only increased my client's anger at the situation.

Great, I thought, now my client and the pilots are falling out with each other, and I am going to be left stranded in Mwanza.

After some further heated exchanges between them, my client agreed to the increased rate, and the pilots returned to the terminal building to see what our options were. They soon came back with a proposal. The air traffic control officials had agreed that we could depart from Mwanza; however, once our plane had left the runway, they would switch off the runway lights, which meant that we could not return to the airport in the event of an emergency or in case the Ugandan authorities refused us permission to land. On balance, we decided that this seemed to be a sensible solution, so we got back on board and taxied out for take-off.

The pilots told us not to disturb them once we were airborne as they would be flying by instruments only. It was pitch black outside now, so there was no horizon to get a bearing. They had to be focused to ensure that the aircraft was flying level and in the right direction. Flying at night creates odd sensations, a feeling that you are descending when you are in fact ascending, and vice versa. Planes have been known to crash as a result. We were more than happy to let them fly undisturbed.

As we lifted off, I looked back, and true to their word, air traffic control turned off the runway lights. We were now on our own in the night sky.

We flew north in silence with only the lights of the plane's instrument panel illuminating the cabin. Eventually, the twinkling lights of Entebbe could be seen ahead of us. As we approached the airport, one of our pilots pointed to something to our right. In the distance, we could see the flashing lights of another plane. The pilot said that this was the evening flight coming in from Brussels. We were cleared to land after it, so we held our course and altitude as the giant aircraft turned behind us and then descended below us to land. We continued over the runway and then banked in a wide loop to our left until we were back on final approach. We were cleared to land and shortly pulled up in front of the terminal building. We went through the immigration channel unchallenged and headed out to our car outside. A long and eventful day was finally at an end.

As we drove back into Kampala, I reflected on the fact that I never got that Tanzanian exit stamp in my passport at Mwanza, and was now technically an illegal immigrant in Tanzania. I wonder if they are still looking for me!

Chapter 12

Highway to Hell

A year later I found myself once again flying back to Uganda. I had been asked to meet with the son of a Kenyan Asian businessman to discuss possible financing for his family's cotton business in Uganda and Tanzania. The plan was to meet his son in Kampala, drive to Mbale to look at a cotton gin they had bought there and then continue over the border to Nakuru in Kenya, where the family business was based. I would meet with the businessman there before heading off the next day to Musoma in Tanzania.

I waited at the Sheraton Hotel in Kampala all morning for the son to arrive. Hours late, he finally arrived, apologising profusely, as we headed to his waiting car. He had been delayed on family business in Kampala. He put my suitcase into the back of his Mercedes 190 and told his driver to head for Jinja. I was a little concerned that we had a long drive ahead of us to Nakuru and were leaving it rather late, but he seemed relaxed. At Jinja, we headed to Mbale and the cotton gin. It turned out that what they had bought was a large old warehouse with a lot of rusty and dismantled equipment strewn across the floor. This didn't look promising at all. After what I deemed a sufficient amount of time feigning interest in the place, I suggested that we should get moving. The Kenyan border crossing was extremely busy, with trucks of all sizes carrying all manner of cargo to and from Mombasa on the coast waiting to cross. It took some time to get through the passport formalities, but we were finally waved through and carried on our way towards Eldoret, the next big town on the road to Nakuru.

The sun was just beginning to set as we headed east, and night had fallen by the time we reached Eldoret. We stopped at a local hotel for a quick comfort break and to stretch our legs. As we set off on our final leg, my companion decided that he would drive, on the basis that his driver's eyesight was too poor for night driving. We had driven for perhaps thirty minutes before he decided that he urgently needed to use a bathroom. So, we turned around and headed back into the city to the hotel to use its facilities again. At this rate, this was going to be a very long drive!

Back on the road, we headed into the Kenyan highlands. To our north, I could see violent flashes of lightning against the pitch-black sky and hear rumblings of thunder getting progressively closer. All too soon the storm was directly over us, and we found ourselves driving through sheets of torrential rain interspersed with bolts of lightning and thunder overhead. I could just about make out the road in front of us in the headlights of the car and the lumbering overloaded trucks that appeared ahead of us, ghost-like out of the darkness—many without taillights. Given the poor visibility, overtaking them was always an act of faith, with a prayer that nothing was coming from the other direction. The situation was further complicated by the massive potholes in the road. The combination of a major storm overhead, unlit trucks, and a heavily potholed road did not inspire confidence, and I began to feel quite uneasy about reaching Nakuru in one piece. I couldn't help thinking that if we were to break down or have an accident in this weather, our options were limited to staying in the car and potentially getting robbed, or leaving the car and making a tasty dinner for the wild animals lurking out there in the bush! To make matters worse, we had absolutely no means to call for assistance!

It was with a great sigh of relief, and a silent prayer of thanks, that we reached Nakuru safely that evening. We had a very late dinner at a local restaurant with my companion's father and older brother, before returning to the family home well after midnight. After a little whiskey nightcap, I settled down in a guestroom for the night to try and get some sleep. We had an early start in the morning on the next leg, a five-hour drive to Musoma across the border in Tanzania.

Up at dawn, I was pleased to discover that we would be going in a Toyota Land Cruiser rather than the small Mercedes. Even better, I was offered the front seat as the father and his two sons settled into the back seat. The drive took us back towards Eldoret before we turned off at Kisumu and headed into the highlands famous for its tea estates and scenery reminiscent of England. The road for much of the way was every bit as potholed as our drive the previous evening, and I was being tossed around as we headed south to the border. Despite this, I would find myself dozing off at intervals only to be interrupted by one or the other of the back seat passengers poking their head forward to ask whether I thought they might qualify for a loan from the bank.

This was going to be a long drive. I resigned myself to having to deal with their questions as we went. At least when we arrived in Musoma I would be joined by a South African colleague, Richard, who was driving up from Mwanza to meet us at the cotton plant. If there was business to do locally in Tanzania with this family, then he would have to take responsibility for it! The plan was that I would return to Mwanza with him, fly on to Dar es Salaam and ultimately home to London.

We carried on slowly until we finally arrived in Musoma, my ears ringing from the incessant questions coming from the back seat, my bones rattling about from the battering my body was taking. We pulled up at a large factory and I was delighted to find my colleague waiting for us. We spent the next couple of hours touring the plant, until it was finally time to say our goodbyes. I left my companions with faint encouragement that we might be able to work together in the future and gratefully climbed into my colleague's 4x4 for the drive to Mwanza.

It was going to be another long drive taking us along

the edge of the Serengeti National Park. As we set off, Richard reached behind, opened a coolbox and pulled out two cold beers. Pure nectar after a hot and dusty factory tour! Soon we were opening a second and settling in for the drive south. Richard had arranged for us to stay at a small "hotel" on the shores of Lake Victoria for the night, as it would be dark before we got to Mwanza, making it too dangerous to drive given the poor state of the road.

Three hours later, we pulled off the main road and headed to the Lake and our overnight stop. The "hotel" had been built by a young Dutch couple who had been travelling through East Africa on motorbike. They had come across the spot by the Lake and fallen in love with it. As a result, they stayed and had set up an overnight campsite for fellow travellers passing through Tanzania. It had since expanded, and now not only catered for the gap year crowd—charging five dollars a night for a simple shelter under which they could pitch a tent—but they had also built six beautiful rondavels, traditional South African circular thatched huts for the more discerning customer. Each was beautifully constructed in stone with a large luxury bed, shower, toilet, and lounge seats inside, all for just twenty-five dollars a night.

The main building had a lakeside bar and restaurant and was set on the shore with stunning views across the Lake. I knew I was going to enjoy this overnight stopover. We took drinks on the terrace as the sun was setting in the west, but were soon forced inside by the thousands of lake flies swarming along the shoreline.

Dinner itself was excellent fare, accompanied by a very agreeable South African red wine. Naturally, I offered to pay for dinner and the two rooms, with the bill for the night coming to a grand total of one hundred dollars. An amazing place at an amazing price, well off the beaten track!

Well rested, we set off that Sunday morning on the last bone-jarring leg to Mwanza. The sun was up, it was hot, and there was little other traffic on what was really a dried track with deep wheel ruts cut into it from the rainy season. We bounced and twisted along the road until, finally, through the sunny haze, Mwanza appeared, a welcome sight for two hot, sweaty, and aching travellers. We headed for the main hotel in town, the Tilapia Hotel, where Richard had booked me a room for the night.

The Tilapia was well known in Mwanza for two things, its Sunday brunch, where mainly expatriate families came to spend the day lounging by the pool; and its houseboat, the African Queen, moored on the lakeshore. It was claimed that the houseboat had starred in the movie of the same name with Humphrey Bogart, and it was now a floating wing of the hotel with seven bedrooms.

I had a room on the boat, which was something to look forward to. I hadn't slept on a houseboat since the early 1970s, when our family would spend summers on a houseboat on Lake Dal in Srinagar in Kashmir. I had many happy memories of that time.

I joined my colleague at the poolside bar for a cold beer. The place was busy, and my colleague seemed to know many of those present. A group of ten burly men were drinking at the bar and we joined them. They were a mix of Australians and South Africans, gold miners working at the Bulyanhulu Gold Mine further south. They had just spent the last month working at the mine, so this was their first weekend off, and they had been making the most of it! Many had ZZ Top style beards of varying lengths and were downing beers at an alarming rate in the hot afternoon sun. After about an hour, Richard headed home, leaving me in the company of the miners.

At one point a particularly tough looking Australian, bearded and with a shaved head, looking a little worse for wear, took exception to my rather stylish green German glasses. In his opinion they were a little on the feminine side—to put it politely. To be fair, they were probably a bit too unusual for the African bush, but they were all I had. For a moment, I thought that this was where things kicked off, but laughing and agreeing that they were less than practical, I managed to move the conversation on to another subject. As I was a banker, he wanted my opinion on where and how he should invest his hard-earned money. He had worked in some of the most inhospitable mining territories on earth—Australia, Papua New Guinea, and Africa, and consequently had saved a significant sum of money. He kept his money with Citibank, but felt that he wasn't getting enough value for it. I now had the surreal experience of discussing investment options (and I was certainly no expert on the matter) on the shore of Lake Victoria after a long day, drinking in the hot sun with a tough miner.

I must have made some sense, as he seemed to accept my advice, or perhaps, as we were both just too far gone, any nonsense made sense at that stage. By the time I finally stumbled off to find my room on the boat, we departed as the best of friends! They were heading back to work the next morning but carried on drinking into the early hours.

I fell into bed marvelling at the collection of people I had just spent the day with but looking forward to getting back to civilization the next day after a long and painful trip around Lake Victoria.

And after all that, we never did finance that company in Nakuru, and I never came across that Australian miner again. I just hope that he is retired and enjoying his well-earned savings.

Chapter 13

Mike Tyson, Goldilocks, and Me

In 1997, I joined a colleague on a business trip to Nigeria, my first visit to the country. Always happy to hop on a plane to experience new cultures, I had readily jumped at the opportunity to go. I had heard so many stories, mainly bad, about Nigeria that I was keen to see it for myself. My only concern with the date of travel was that I would be flying to Lagos the day after a wedding I was attending in Yorkshire. I would have to fly from Manchester to Amsterdam to connect with the flight to Lagos.

The morning after the wedding, I managed to wake very early for my taxi to the airport, feeling rather worse for wear. It had been a great evening and I had enjoyed myself, perhaps a little too much. I met up with my colleague in Amsterdam and was surprised to find that he had been booked in economy whilst I was in business class for the flight to Lagos.

I was still feeling a little delicate as we descended towards Lagos that evening. On disembarking, I was assaulted by the oppressive humidity and began to sweat heavily. My colleague, Mike, had managed to work his way forward in time to join me as we walked towards the first line of waiting officials, no doubt ready to pounce on a virgin visitor such as myself! The rivers of sweat running down my face and my increasingly damp shirt must have been red flags to them, marking me out amongst the passengers filing past. Murtala Mohammed International Airport was notorious, certainly at that time, for the picket lines of officials waiting to pounce and "fine" you, perhaps due to a "missing" page in your passport; the "missing" page being a crisp USD bank note. I rightly suspected that in my condition, I would not pass unnoticed.

An official pointed to me and motioned me to one side. Mike had thankfully stayed with me and began to talk to the official. Mike was a well-built Ugandan, with biceps the size of a man's thigh, and bore an uncanny resemblance to the boxer, Mike Tyson. He was often mistaken for him, and the official duly remarked on his resemblance.

"Yes, I am Mike Tyson!" he replied laughing, playing up to the role and he soon had the officials laughing and slapping him on the back, enjoying their moment of fame.

"Mike Tyson" introduced me as his "white brother", also called Mike, which amused them even more. With handshakes all round, they waved us on, with no "missing" pages discovered in our passport.

We carried on through the terminal without further hassle, collected our bags, and located our driver waiting outside. Mike had arranged for us to stay in an apartment in the Apapa district of Lagos. The apartment was owned by a shipping company that he had done some business with before. After a long drive into Lagos from the airport, we finally arrived at around 11 pm. My first impression of our accommodation was favourable: it had a large open plan dining and lounge area, a kitchen and three ensuite bedrooms down the hall. It was late and we were very hungry, so our driver drove us to a nearby Chinese restaurant for a late dinner, where we were entertained by the only other diners in the room, a group of Chinese men drunkenly singing karaoke, rather off-key!

Returning to the apartment, we had a couple of beers as a nightcap, before turning in for the night. We had a busy schedule the next day, although I was surprised that there was so much time allocated between each meeting. I realised why it was so the next morning as we headed off to our first meeting. Soon, we joined a chaotic mass of vehicles, belching fumes, somehow slowly moving in one direction or the other, even if it meant driving on the wrong side of the road! This was no rush hour traffic; this was an all-day Lagos experience! It would take hours to negotiate our way around Lagos, hence the big gaps between meetings. Moving along in the slow-moving traffic, I realised that Lagos was one of three cities—the others being Moscow and Sao Paulo—where I had no real sense of direction, where it was impossible to picture where we were on a mental map of the city.

Our first meeting was at a cocoa processing plant in Ikeja. We were shown to the Managing Director's large office on arrival. I was starting to feel a little queasy from the previous night's mix of Chinese food and Nigerian beer as my body began sending me increasingly urgent messages that a comfort break was needed and needed fast.

Introductions made, I asked the Managing Director if it might be possible to use a washroom. Expecting to be directed down the corridor, he instead opened a door set in the wood panelled wall of his office, revealing his own private washroom. I had no other choice but to use it. I entered the small room and went about my business, hoping that the walls were thick enough to muffle any embarrassing noises to those in the office outside.

Refreshed, I returned to the meeting. As I took my seat, Mike quickly excused himself and disappeared into the washroom. As the Managing Director and I engaged in several minutes of small talk, our conversation was accompanied by a series of loud thunderclaps from the other side of the wall. Clearly, the walls weren't quite as thick as I had hoped! My colleague returned and took his seat, both of us silently hoping that our host would not need to use his washroom any time soon. I suspect that he may have regretted his decision to allow us to use his personal washroom, and had probably made a mental note to have it thoroughly fumigated once we had departed!

We spent the rest of the morning learning about how Nigerian cocoa powder, cocoa butter and cocoa oil is made from cocoa beans and the remainder of the day moving from one meeting to the next, until we finally returned to our apartment, exhausted. There was one further washroom emergency call later in the day. We found ourselves in a building near the port using a rather more rudimentary facility, one requiring a good sense of balance and an ability to hold one's breath for a sufficient period. An executive's washroom it certainly was not! An important aspect of international travel I had learned early in my career was to always ensure one had a roll of toilet paper in your bag for such emergencies!

That evening, we were invited to dinner at the Lagos Yacht Club in Ikoyi. The meal was excellent and the surroundings very pleasant, a haven of peace in the surrounding chaos. However, our expatriate host, the Country Head of the bank we worked for, was very keen to stress that Lagos was a dangerous city, particularly when out on the roads at night. He wanted to make sure that we headed back to our apartment early enough to avoid any potential problems. By 9 pm, we were back in our car and heading back to the apartment. As it happened, we were stopped at a military roadblock. A soldier popped his head in the window and, on initially seeing just Mike sitting in the back, looked like he was going to make things a little difficult. But then he noticed me, and perhaps mindful of the size of my colleague (looking his most Mike Tyson), waved us on our way without any further hassle.

It was still relatively early when we got back, and we decided to enjoy a few more beers. I was temporarily baffled by the fact that there were already a couple of empty beer bottles on the table which I didn't recall drinking earlier. And the television didn't work either, when it had done the previous evening. No worries, it wasn't important; and we were setting the world to rights over our beers when we finally called it a night.

The following morning, I awoke to the sound of voices in the apartment. I assumed that Mike had arranged for one of his clients to meet us here and had simply neglected to mention it to me. I poked my head out the bedroom door and noticed that the door to one of the two bedrooms opposite was open. The two beds in it had clearly been slept in but there was no sign of Mike. I opened the door to the third room and found him fast asleep in the bed.

Having had quite a lot to drink the previous night, I assumed that Mike had wandered during the night and ended up bed hopping between the two bedrooms. I could still hear the voices coming from the living room and decided to investigate.

To my surprise there were two Indian men sitting at the table eating their breakfast! They were equally surprised at seeing me and after mumbling a quick good morning, I retreated down the hallway to wake Mike with the news that we seemed to have acquired two mystery guests overnight!

We returned to the living room to ask who they were and more importantly what they were doing in our apartment? It turned out they were the captain and first officer of a container ship that had docked in Lagos port the previous night. The shipping company had provided them with overnight accommodation in the company apartment, it just so happened to be the same apartment we were in!

They had arrived when we were at the Yacht Club and had been asleep when we got back. It was a bit disconcerting to realise that there had been two strange men in our apartment all night and we had been none the wiser. It also explained the mystery of the empty beer bottles and the television not working when we had returned! Mystery solved, we joined them for breakfast before going our separate ways; they went back to their ship and we went on to our final meetings.

Chapter 14

The Cotton Club

People may not know that Burkina Faso, Benin, and Togo are major producers and exporters of cotton in West Africa. I had been discussing a potential cotton financing with a Belgian trading company who bought their cotton from these countries. We agreed that a visit to meet the state-owned cotton producers in each was the next logical step. I was excited at the prospect of visiting the three, generally off the beaten track for most business travellers.

A few weeks later, we flew into Ouagadougou on an Air France flight from Paris, having briefly stopped in Bamako, Mali, en route. We would stay one day in the capital for meetings before flying on to Bobo-Dioulasso, the cotton capital in the west of the country. I spent my day in Ouagadougou meeting with local banks, an interesting test of my French language skills, but somehow, I got through it no worse for wear.

The next morning, we flew to Bobo-Dioulasso and booked into the only hotel of note in town, the

L'Auberge. The rooms were plain but clean and thankfully had air conditioning. There was a large terrace at the front of the hotel facing the main street.

It was on the terrace that I encountered the German tradition of Stammtisch played out in West Africa! I knew about it in Germany but had not expected to find it practised in Burkina Faso. By way of background, my brother had worked in Bavaria some years before and had been living in a small town, Sulzdorf, near Wurzburg. He was put up in a small hotel in the town which had a bar and restaurant downstairs. The place was very popular in the evenings with the locals, who would come in after a day's work to eat and drink, and consequently, it would get quite busy. One evening, my brother came down from his room for dinner to find the place packed. Luckily for him, there was an empty table close to the bar. Naturally, he worked his way through the crowd and took a seat, no doubt congratulating himself on his good fortune.

The bar went quiet as people realised he was sitting at the empty table. The barman came over and told him that he couldn't sit there. This was the Stammtisch table! My brother, not being familiar with the term, wondered what he meant.

In many Bavarian restaurants or beer halls, there will be a table placed conveniently near the bar surrounded by empty chairs. There may even be a sign hanging above saying Stammtisch. Sitting at a Stammtisch table is a privilege reserved for the very best regulars. They are invitation-only, intensely territorial, and strictly male. The barman explained this table was the Stammtisch table, reserved for his local regulars; one could only sit at it by invitation from one of them.

Not wishing to upset local custom, my brother moved from the table. Over time as he became a more familiar face in the bar, he was eventually invited to join the Stammtisch table and sit with the regulars. And that is how I came to know of the Stammtisch tradition.

What relevance does this have to Bobo-Dioulasso? My client and I had gone to sit on the hotel terrace on our first evening to have a beer. There were several empty tables, and I went to sit at one I considered the best place to view the comings and goings on the street. My companion suggested it might be better if we sat at one of the many other empty tables instead. He explained that this specific table was a Stammtisch table. A little later an elderly German man came in off the street and took his place at the table where he was soon joined by three elderly Burkinabé men, clearly all good friends. Drinks ordered, they settled down to a lively discussion.

Here was the Stammtisch tradition, alive and well, thousands of miles from home, in the heat and dust of Bobo-Dioulasso, in Burkina Faso!

We finished our beers, bade good evening to the Stammtisch table, and headed out to dinner. We were going to walk to a restaurant, quite a novelty in Africa. In other parts of the continent, we might have been mugged or worse within five minutes of leaving our hotel at night on foot. In western Burkina Faso however, it felt quite safe and natural as we walked along the dusty streets without any bother.

As we strolled to the restaurant my companion mentioned that I "should be prepared to sing for my supper" that night. I wasn't quite sure what he meant, but was looking forward to a good meal to finish off the day. We turned into a side street and came to a walled compound, illuminated by a string of coloured lights running across the top of the wall. I could hear soft classical music coming from within. We entered through a gate into a small courtyard where about fifteen tables were set. In one corner of the courtyard was a large statue of Jesus, beside a small fountain, arms outstretched, looking benevolently down on us. The restaurant was run by women dressed in traditional brightly coloured African print wrap dresses. It was a simple but serene setting, with the soft music playing in the background. As we took out seats, my companion explained that the women were in fact nuns. The restaurant was their means of funding their work in the community, caring for the handicapped and impoverished of the city.

We enjoyed a lovely dinner, serenaded by the classical music playing softly in the background. After we had finished the main course, the music was turned off and the nuns circulated amongst the tables handing out song sheets to the diners. A nun took up station by each table and they began to sing Ave Maria. It was the most beautiful singing I had heard for some time. We were encouraged to join in, and many did, but I couldn't bring myself to add my tuneless voice to such a beautiful and harmonious rendition and simply mouthed along silently. For about ten minutes it was the most peaceful place—heaven on earth.

When they finished singing, the song sheets were collected, and we continued our meal, feeling rather humbled by the experience. I now knew what my companion had meant about singing for my supper! For all my travels around Africa, it was probably the one experience that was both unexpected and beautiful and has remained one of my favourite memories of the continent.

Our original itinerary after we finished our meetings was to fly from Bobo-Dioulasso to Cotonou, Benin for meetings and then fly from Cotonou to Lomé, Togo before flying home from Lomé. However, our flight to Cotonou was cancelled at short notice and our only option was to drive back to Ouagadougou and catch a flight from there the next day, if possible. The only flight available was to Lomé, which meant that we would have to change our plans and drive from Lomé to Cotonou and then come back to Lomé for my flight back to Amsterdam. I had one small problem with this revised itinerary. I only had a single-entry visa for Togo and would now be entering the country twice. It would be interesting to see how that played out with the immigration authorities.

We flew on an Air Burkina DC9 which had clearly seen better days, but it thankfully got us to Lomé in one piece. We were met by our driver and set off for Cotonou, arriving at the border in good time. As with most borders we were held up by petty bureaucracy for a couple of hours before having our passports stamped, and then we were on our way again.

We spent two nights in Cotonou meeting cotton traders and the state-owned cotton marketing board. We stayed in the Novotel which had a nightclub/karaoke bar in the basement, whose only patrons appeared to be a group of Lebanese men and their girlfriends. One of the women, heavily made up and tottering on impossibly high heels, would screech along to the songs in Arabic, which was the cue for us to finish our drinks and move on.

The drive back to Lomé passed without incident and I crossed the border again, illegally entering Togo for the second time, without hindrance. I bade farewell to my client from Belgium at that point and waited at the hotel to meet another cotton trading client who had flown in from the UK. He had arranged meetings in Lomé and a site visit to a cotton ginnery up country. Once again, I managed to get myself through a day of meetings in French before we headed north to visit the gin the next morning. We spent the morning at the site before wrapping things up in the early afternoon. I was flying back to Amsterdam that evening, so I wanted to ensure we were back in Lomé in good time. However, my client's local agent was very keen for us to make a stop at his mother's house to pay our respects before we left. We agreed and the driver took a detour through the back streets until we came to a small house.

We were met by an elderly grey-haired woman who ushered us into a small room with a sofa and armchair. She offered us some local pastries and drinks and handed us a couple of chipped enamel mugs to drink from. My client was a young, rather timid, Frenchman, who seemed rather ill at ease in this setting. He politely refused all offerings of food or water, no doubt afraid he might pick up some nasty bug. I, on the other hand, heartily accepted the food and water out of courtesy and ate and drank both. To be fair, for a moment I did have a fleeting thought that if I had a reaction to the water later, I would probably be sitting in the aircraft toilet rather than in my seat for the long flight home . But I felt that it was a small price to pay rather than insult the old lady by not accepting her hospitality.

We bade our farewells and headed back to Lomé to collect my belongings and head to the airport that evening. I was concerned that I might be stopped at passport control and had an argument ready in my mind along the lines of having no wish to remain in Togo, but thankfully no one spotted the visa anomaly, and I departed that evening on KLM as planned. Another three countries in Africa were added to my list! And I didn't end up on the toilet seat flying home either!

Chapter 15

Parting Memories

As my career changed direction in 2003, I had to say goodbye to Africa and move on to pastures new. Over the years of travelling to different parts of the continent I had seen and experienced many wonderful, amusing and occasionally dangerous situations.

A South African colleague in London asked to join me on a trip I was taking to Kenya, Tanzania, and Uganda. I would fly into Nairobi on a Sunday and my colleague would join me the following day.

He arrived at the hotel that Monday as planned. I waited for him in the bar while he went to check in. Half an hour later, he returned, looking rather pleased with himself. He remarked on how impressed he was with the hotel and his room. To be honest, I thought it was a nice hotel, but nothing struck me as special, so I was surprised at how excited he was with it. He explained that he had told the staff at the reception that he worked for the Standard Bank Group of South Africa. When he entered his room, the hotel attendant had turned on the television, and there in the corner of the screen was the Standard Bank logo! He was impressed that the hotel had put the logo on the screen in his honour!

Thinking that this was rather odd, I asked if there was any sport on at the time.

"Actually, yes," he replied, "Cricket!"

"Alright, the cricket is on MNET, the South African sports channel, which is sponsored by the bank, hence the logo on the screen!"

I think he was disappointed to find out it hadn't been done for him!

I then asked him what meetings he had arranged in Nairobi. His first meeting was at the Central Bank that afternoon, he said.

"That's strange," I said, "The Central Bank is closed as it is hosting a lunch for President Arap Moi today."

No, he was quite adamant, he had a confirmed meeting that afternoon at 3 pm at the KCB, the Kenyan Central Bank. I patiently explained that the KCB was in fact the Kenya Commercial Bank and not the Central Bank which was the CBK! After lunch, I put him in a taxi to the KCB and waved him off with a heavy heart, wondering how this man was going to survive the day, let alone the week in Africa!

That evening we went to dinner at The Carnivore, a popular and well-known outdoor restaurant in Nairobi. It specialised in all sorts of barbequed meat, from the exotic ones such as ostrich, antelope, zebra and crocodile to more traditional fare such as chicken, lamb and pork. The meat was roasted on

Masai spears in large charcoal pits that dominated the place. It was very much a forerunner of the famous Brazilian churrascaria restaurants popular in London today. Accompanying the food was The Carnivore's famous Dawa cocktail, again very similar to the caipirinha from Brazil, on which it was based. Cane sugar, lime and ice all mashed together, and very nice it was too! A flag was placed on the table by the staff, and if the flag kept flying the waiters kept coming with skewers of food.

During the evening, my rookie South African asked how they got the animals on to the spears for roasting in the pits. Unable to resist, I explained that they were backed up towards the pits where the cooks lay in wait with their spears. The animals were impaled on them and quickly flipped over into the pit in one swift motion! Simple, really! My colleague almost bought the story, he really was that naïve!

The next day we flew to Dar es Salaam in Tanzania. After a day of meetings, we arranged to have dinner with our local colleagues at the Yacht Club. On the drive there, they suggested that we stop at a popular roadside bar called Mary's for a cold beer. Mary reputedly sold the coldest beer in town out of her little roadside shack or duka, as they were known. We pulled over to the side of the road and enjoyed a few Castle's, as cold as promised. Each duka on the road sold a specific product, be it vegetables, fruit, or cuts of meat. My colleague looked quite ill at ease standing on the side of the road drinking beer and mingling with the locals. Not something he would have done in South Africa for sure! When I heard him ask if the shopkeepers had checkout machines and bar code readers in their little dukas, I knew this man was not for Africa.

The next morning, I flew to Arusha in the north of the country with a couple of my local colleagues for meetings for the day. One of the meetings was with the CEO of Precision Air, a new private airline in Tanzania. The CEO was confident of the success of his airline, given Air Tanzania's unreliability and record for cancelling flights. When we arrived back at the airport for our return flight, we were told that our Air Tanzania flight had been cancelled. This was a problem, as we were due to fly on to Uganda the next morning. I needed to get back to Dar that night and my colleagues went off in search of some alternative means of transport. I found three English businessmen hanging around looking a bit lost as to what to do, and got talking to them. They were also trying to get back to Dar, so I told them that they were welcome to join us if we found some means of getting there. I even managed to visit the air traffic control tower, which had an amazing clear view to the snow-capped Mount Kilimanjaro in the distance.

My colleagues eventually returned. They had been able to charter a private plane to get us back, but it would cost four hundred dollars. Out of the six of us, I was the only one who had that amount of cash on me, so I would have to pay for the flight. An hour later, the pilot arrived, with his wife in tow for company for the return flight, and we went out to a small plane on the tarmac.

I paid the pilot, and he signed the back of one of my business cards as evidence of the payment. I hoped that it would suffice when I submitted my expenses on my return to London. One of my colleagues had thankfully bought a case of beer to ease the journey south as night fell. We flew in total darkness, the light from the cockpit dials our sole illumination in the cabin. With little else to do, the six of us worked our way through the case of beer. As we began to approach Dar, the pilot informed us that we needed to circle to allow other commercial air traffic to land first. This was not helpful, as we were all now beginning to feel the effects of the beer and needed a toilet break. Unfortunately, there wasn't one on board, and we would have to wait until we landed.

We finally landed and taxied to the terminal building, with the six of us lined up at the door like a stick of skydivers waiting to jump, desperate to get off and get to a toilet before one of us had an embarrassing accident. Anyone watching must have thought it a bizarre sight as six grown men launched themselves out of the aircraft as it came to a stop and sprinted into the building. Thankfully, there was a toilet just inside the building, and soon, we were all emitting groans of relief, much to the amusement of the cleaning ladies waiting outside!

I was asleep in my business class seat on the Kenya Airways Sunday night flight from London to Nairobi when I was woken up by an announcement from the captain. There was a technical problem with the aircraft causing an unequal flow of fuel between the two engines. We were currently over Egypt, and there were two possible solutions. We could descend to a lower altitude and continue flying, but we would be heading into Sudanese air space. If the problem worsened, he wasn't confident that we could resolve it if we had to make an emergency landing in Khartoum. The alternative was to land at the nearest airport in Egypt and get it fixed there. However, Cairo Airport was closed due to a sandstorm, which meant the nearest place we could land was Luxor; and so this is where we would head.

We descended towards Luxor and landed at 5 am in the morning. As we taxied to a stop in front of the terminal the captain announced that the terminal was currently closed, and we would have to sit in the aircraft until it opened in a few hours. Despite the early hour, it was becoming increasingly hot in the cabin, so the doors were left open, and the crew opened the drink trolleys for us to help ourselves. I started talking to the captain, who confirmed that he had managed to contact the Kenya Airways office in Cairo to let London and Nairobi know where we were. However, the part that was needed to fix the engine problem would have to be flown down from Cairo once the weather cleared, so we were likely to be in Luxor for the day, at least.

After a further hour or so, our captain announced that the crew had managed to find accommodation for us at a hotel in Luxor for the day until the replacement part arrived. I was travelling in my suit and, given the heat outside, had no choice but to buy a t-shirt in the terminal, which cost me fifteen dollars! Probably the most expensive t-shirt I have ever bought!

Passports stamped, we were taken by bus to a rather pleasant hotel in Luxor on the banks of the Nile and settled in for the day to try and catch up on some sleep. I rang my London office to let them know where I was, having suddenly disappeared off the face of the earth halfway through the flight to Nairobi.

I had got to know my fellow business class passengers rather well by now, so we decided that we might as well enjoy a Nile cruise. We headed down to the river and hired a felucca, loaded up with some beer, and set off down the Nile enjoying a spectacular sunset along the way, me wearing my suit trousers and my recently purchased t-shirt. After that there was nothing more to do but relax at the hotel in our rooms that evening and wait.

Finally, at 3 am, we were called down to the lobby and driven back to the airport. The fault had been fixed, and we were soon on our way to Nairobi, having enjoyed our unscheduled and unexpected holiday in Luxor courtesy of Kenya Airways!

What a small world it is. I was in Brazzaville, Republic of Congo, with a former colleague from Zambia, now working for another Bank in London. A group of us were working on a big financing for the national oil company in Congo and were in town as part of our due diligence process. My former colleague, Keith, and I were delegated to fly to Pointe Noire on the coast to visit the oil refinery. A small private jet had been laid on to get us there. We headed out to the airport where our pilots were waiting for us. The captain was a South African, and the co-pilot, a female pilot from England. It was a short flight to the coast, and once we had disembarked, we headed off in a 4x4 to the oil refinery which was operated by Total, the French oil company. The pilots remained at the airport for our return in a couple of hours.

When we arrived at the oil refinery gates, we were stopped by the security and advised that we were not on the list of expected visitors. We would not be allowed to enter. This was, to put it mildly, a bit of a surprise, but no amount of argument would make them budge. We had no alternative but to return to the airport with our tails between our legs.

At the airport our pilots gave us the bad news that the airport was now closed for the rest of the afternoon, and we were stuck in Pointe Noire until the evening before we could depart. The President had flown in on an official visit, so we had no alternative but to head back into town and wait. We decided that all four of us might as well get some lunch and went to a nice beachside restaurant, where we enjoyed a long slow lunch in the sun, with the waves of the Atlantic lapping gently on to the beach beside us.

The female pilot and Keith got talking about life in Africa. He told her that he was Zambian and to his surprise, she told him that she had also grown up in Zambia. As they explored their newfound common heritage in more detail, it became clear that they had known each other as children in Zambia. She then said that she was heading back to the UK the following week for her father's wedding. She casually mentioned that her father's best man was an ex Irish rugby international, and being Irish myself, I asked her who that was. She said that he was a former prop called Gary Halpin. Well, imagine her surprise when I told her that I had been to school with Gary Halpin! He had been a couple of years behind me, but his older brother, John, had been in my year. I don't think she could ever have imagined sitting with two strangers she had just met that day, in a beachside restaurant in Congo, who both had a connection to her!

Back in Brazzaville, we met up with our colleagues that night for dinner. The next day was spent working but that evening my French colleague expressed an interest in experiencing some of the nightlife that Brazzaville had to offer. I agreed to join him, and we jumped into a taxi. Our driver took us down to the river and dropped us outside an apartment block where there was a nightclub on the roof. We took the lift to the top floor and entered the club. It had a great view of Kinshasa, lit up at night on the other side of the river. It felt quite strange to be looking across at the city where I had spent two years of my life and where some of my good friends were still based.

We sat at a table and ordered two large bottles of Primus beer. Looking around us, it was clear we were the only foreigners in the club. We drank our beers, enjoying the Congolese beats and cool breeze coming in off the river. Soon enough, the ladies in the club who had been watching us began to come over and join us at our table. Eventually the moment arrived where they wanted us to dance with them. My colleague and I were quite happy to do so and joined them on the dance floor. To our horror, it turned out that my colleague's dance form was quite eclectic. He was quite tall and thin with large feet. His dance style combined the movements of a praying mantis with all the characteristics of Mr Bean on a dance floor, arms and legs moving in all sorts of directions and with no sense of rhythm. Our dance companions had seen enough, and promptly left us alone on the dance floor rather than risk injury amongst the flailing arms and legs. I swiftly joined them. I cannot ever recall seeing such a thing happen before. My colleague returned to our table where we finished our beers and decided to head home.

Zimbabwe was always one of my favourite destinations in Africa. It was always a haven of safety and order on the continent compared to the chaos around it. My first visit in 1992 to Harare felt like a step back in time to the 1950s with its older model cars and department stores straight out of the Are You Being Served era! Of course, the city and country had modernised quickly since that initial visit.

Harare was one city in Africa where you could walk the streets safely at any time of the day and night, where the people were well educated, friendly and had moved on from the apartheid years of the Smith era. I had visited many times on business since and took Fiona there for our honeymoon in 1993. We had spent ten days at Victoria Falls and

Hwange National Park on safari followed by a stay at the famous Troutbeck Inn in the Eastern Highlands. Indeed, one of the highlights of our stay was to hire a battered old taxi at Victoria Falls to take us to our next venue at Hwange which was three hours away! Many a colleague in Harare dined out on that story for years after. It would have been cheaper to buy the car!

Zimbabwe was the complete opposite to what I experienced in Kinshasa. The economy was strongly driven by exports of tobacco, gold, beef, and agricultural products, and from tourism and mining. The currency was stable, the politics progressive and life was generally comfortable, which couldn't be said for Kinshasa. Unfortunately, over the subsequent years, the politics became less inclusive and more extremist, resulting in the ruling party destroying its own economy and currency through land seizures. By the time of my last visit to Zimbabwe in 2006, Harare had become Kinshasa, with a rapidly devaluating and worthless currency, where dollars were extremely difficult to find, and where it no longer felt safe to walk the streets of the city. Tourism had fallen significantly, and hotels had semi-closed down as a result.

Despite the changes, I enjoyed returning to the country. On one of my visits prior to 2006 we spent a few days visiting various tobacco farmers around the country. At the time we financed tobacco exports and Harare had one of the biggest tobacco leaf auction houses in the world. We spent a day at the auction house watching the buyers from the major cigarette manufacturers such as BAT and Universal bidding on bales of tobacco leaf laid out in a huge warehouse. It was staggering to see the sheer volume of tobacco leaf processed through the warehouse daily. Rows upon rows of bales were lined up and the auctioneer would walk along each row with the buyers in tow. They would spend on average ten seconds at each bale bidding and then move on to the next whilst someone behind recorded the sale price and who bought it. I asked how many cigarettes could be made from one 50 kg bale of tobacco leaf. Our guide replied that although not exact, he thought that if a person smoked twenty cigarettes a day, then a bale of tobacco would supply twenty years of his smoking requirements!

Our trip also provided us with the opportunity to spend the weekend in the country. My Harare based Zimbabwean colleague Malcolm suggested we should spend it fishing on Lake Kariba. He said being out on the lake with only the wildlife and the stars for company was a once in a lifetime experience. This sounded like a splendid idea, so arrangements were made and on Friday morning we headed off on the drive northwest to Kariba.

At Kariba, we boarded a boat with two decks. The lower deck contained cabins and a galley and had a cage attached to the stern. This, I was informed, was so kids could swim safely in the lake. The cage would be lowered into the water and the kids would swim inside the cage protecting them from the crocodiles in the water. Given the number of crocodiles in the lake, reckoned to be one for every metre of shoreline, I could see no compelling reason for me to road test the cage, particularly given how shallow the sides appeared when lowered in the water. To my eyes, any crocodile hungry enough could get over those in no time!

We set sail and settled in with beers in hand for a three-hour trip across the lake. It was late afternoon when our pilot gently nudged the bow into the shoreline and dropped anchor. We were now alone in the wild. Everywhere we looked there were crocs in the water, their eyes visible above the water line, waiting to pounce on any unsuspecting prey. Pods of hippo were scattered around, their distinctive grunts piercing the silence of the wild. We sat on the top deck and enjoyed the moment, taking in the scenery. At dusk, a herd of elephants approached the shoreline to drink, followed later by buffaloes. It was magical.

Malcolm explained that one of the joys of being on the lake was to be able to sleep on the top deck under the stars. I found this rather unsettling. Given the amount of alcohol one consumed, I could very easily see myself getting up in the middle of the night to use the loo and stepping over the side of the boat straight into the water and dinner for the crocodiles. I made it very clear that I was having none of that and would be sleeping in a cabin with four solid walls around me. There were after all certain limits to the whole bush experience!

The next morning, we were up and ready to go fishing. The holy grail of fishing in Kariba was to catch a tiger fish, renowned for its fearsome teeth. I of course had never fished before so was the novice as we set out in a little rowing boat. We were looking for specific areas where the tiger fish would feed but needed to be careful that we didn't wander into a pod of hippos. Once we were in place, we would put a worm on a hook and then cast it into the water. In my case I would either mangle the worm trying to put it on the hook or just end up feeding the other fish in the water and come up empty handed. I would then clean my fingers in the water before trying again. That is until I was advised that was not such a good idea as I might find a crocodile attached to my hand! Eventually I did hook a bream—they were plentiful in the water. The tiger fish however proved elusive, and we returned to the mother ship at the end of the day with plenty of bream for supper, ready for another wildlife parade at dusk. And then back to the safety of my cabin ready to repeat the process the next day before sailing back to Kariba. After a magical weekend living in the bush with nature it was time to return to the real world and head home.

Almost twenty-five years after I had stayed at the iconic Victoria Falls Hotel on my honeymoon, I was able to cross over the border from Zambia in November 2019, and spend a day at the Falls again. It was lovely to see, despite all the hardships that Zimbabwe had been through, the hotel remained open and unchanged. Sadly, despite the staff's best efforts to persuade me to stay for dinner when I recounted how I had stayed twenty-five years before, I had to leave and cross back over the border into Zambia, with a promise that I would return one day!

I visited Namibia twice, once to attend a conference

in Windhoek and the other to visit an offshore diamond mining company operating out of Luderitz in the south of the country. Namibia is a former German colony and there remains a strong German feel to the country. The first sign of the Germanic influence was the polka music piped incessantly throughout our hotel. Luderitz has a working port primarily servicing the offshore diamond mining vessels out in the Atlantic Ocean. South of the town is Kolmanskop, a former mining town where diamonds were mined in the southern Namib Desert. This old settlement sprang up in 1908 when diamonds were first discovered and at its height was a booming town boasting elegant homes, a hospital, shops and factories, a casino and swimming club. Its golden period lasted until the 1940s when the supply of diamonds dwindled, and it was eventually abandoned where it succumbed to the shifting desert sands and wind. Today is a deserted ruin perfectly preserved by the weather. We were taken on a tour of Kolmanskop; it was fascinating to see the preserved buildings laid out in neat rows. Years later, I saw a documentary about a desert hyena in Namibia that hunts on the coast and its home was in the deserted town.

The next morning, we were taken to the airfield where we would take a helicopter out to one of the ships offshore. We were given a safety briefing which included what to do if we ditched in the ocean and handed our life jackets. We climbed in and rose into the air. Our pilot decided to take us on a quick tour of the area before we headed out to sea. He wanted to show us some of the human bones that were constantly being exposed by the shifting sands in the desert. Between 1904 and 1908, the Germans had built concentration camps for the Herero and Namaqua indigenous tribes or driven them into the desert to die. Today, it is accepted as one of the earliest instances of genocide. It was sobering to see those human bones lying in the desert and to think of the circumstances in which these people had been held.

In due course we turned west and flew out over the ocean. About five miles from the coast, we approached several ships mining the seabed and prepared to land on one of them. Offshore diamond mining involved mining the seafloor for diamonds where they had been washed into the sea from rivers over thousands of years. We landed on the ship's landing pad and disembarked. The ship had a large, tracked vehicle at its stern which basically looked like the bottom part of a tank had been married to a vacuum cleaner. This tool was lowered to the seabed and an operator on the boat controlled it as it moved across the seabed sucking up the contents. These would be processed on the vessel with the diamonds collected through several screening processes with the waste returned to the sea. Deep in the bowels of the ship we were shown the highly secure diamond processing room where highly trained sorters graded the stones.

We were not allowed into the processing room for obvious reasons, but it was fascinating to see how the whole process worked to get a rough valueless piece of stone off the seabed and ultimately to Antwerp where it might sell for thousands of pounds. Of course, it all worked well in theory until something went wrong. Which it did two years later when the mining tool was lost on the seafloor and the company hit serious financial problems which ended up taking up a lot of my time in resolving. Indeed, I use the experience as a case study in my presentations of how things can go wrong in my business. But that is another story for another time!

I have had many other experiences across Africa; South Africa, Zambia, Mozambique, Cameroon, Cape Verde, and Cote d'Ivoire to name a few but Zaïre, or the Democratic Republic of Congo as it is now, remains one my favourite and most treasured memories of my time spent in the African continent.

PART III

Back to the Future

Chapter 16

Return of the Prodigals

Thirty years almost to the day that my mother had passed away in Jerusalem, I found myself back in the city. My mother had died there at the young age of fifty two in March 1983 after a long struggle with cancer. I was at university in Dublin at the time and had last seen her three months before in December 1982, when I had come home to Jerusalem for the Christmas holidays. My mother had come out of hospital to spend what turned out to be the little time she had left with the family.

It was a difficult time for all of us; my father's way of dealing with the whole cancer thing was to drink. He was a good father, but I believe he suffered from depression, and drinking was his way of coping, or more accurately, of not coping with our mother's cancer. He was never violent or aggressive when he was drinking, but it used to infuriate me; it was like he had given up and didn't care anymore. With hindsight, having myself reached the same age my mother was when she passed away, I can now better understand what he must have been going through emotionally. After my mother's passing, he retired from the United Nations on 30 June 1983 and moved back to Ireland.

The expatriate life that we knew had come to an end. Given that 1983 was long before the internet and email were developed, I immediately lost contact with many of the international friends I had grown up with in Jerusalem. I never truly felt at home in Ireland, and despite having gone to boarding school there, I had always felt on the periphery of things—Irish but not Irish. Even at school, we were viewed as foreign students. It came home to me many years later as I waited for my older brother at Dublin Airport. I had flown in earlier and was waiting for his flight to arrive from Gatwick. I sat with a coffee watching the waiting crowd in the terminal. There were families waiting for their loved ones, many holding welcome home banners and balloons. As sons, daughters, husbands, or wives were spotted coming out of the baggage collection area, shouts of joy, laughter and a few tears would sweep through the crowd. I watched it dispassionately and it occurred to me that I had never experienced that emotion of coming home when I arrived in Dublin, of having returned from my travels to an excited family waiting in anticipation. For all that I loved coming back to Ireland, Jerusalem—to all intents and purposes—was home for me, and Tel Aviv airport was where my parents waited at arrivals twice a year to welcome me home.

I always felt that I had never said a final goodbye to

Jerusalem after my mother's passing and my father's retirement. The suddenness of the change in our lives left me feeling empty, like a chapter in my life remained unfinished. For many years, I felt a strong urge to go back one day, to return with my children to show them where I had been born, grown up, gone to school; but nothing ever came of it. Each year was a case of 'maybe next year', and as the years passed, the thought of returning remained nothing more than an idea lodged in the recesses of my brain.

As it happened, my sister Pamela, living in the USA, had harboured the same desire to show her family where she had grown up. We had discussed going back many times over the years and realised that this longing to return was really something we needed to do for ourselves rather than for our families. And then, the opportunity arose in May 2013 for us to do just that: go back to Jerusalem. We booked our respective flights from London and Philadelphia to Tel Aviv with great excitement. After thirty years, it felt like we were finally going "home"!

My British Airways flight departed from Heathrow late on a Friday night, arriving at Tel Aviv at 5 am the next morning. Pamela's flight was not due into Tel Aviv until later that Saturday afternoon. I had done some preliminary research on how to get to Jerusalem from Tel Aviv, and the quickest and most direct option was to take a taxi.

I barely slept on the flight. I was excited and apprehensive at the same time. What if it was all a major disappointment to me, what if the reality of the place clashed with my memories of our time there? Would we be able to move freely around the city, would we remember and find the places that were dear to us? Would the security situation remain stable during our four days in the city? As my flight approached the Israeli coastline, the onboard flight map swept away any doubts I had, displaying all the names so familiar to me from thirty years ago; Netanya, Haifa, Tel Aviv, Jaffa, Ashkelon, Gaza City. This was it; I was coming back "home"!

I passed through Passport Control without any problems. I had expected to be taken aside given my place of birth recorded on my Irish passport was "Palestine," but apart from being asked the purpose of my visit, it was all rather straightforward. Pleasantly surprised, I exited the terminal building and jumped into the first taxi on the rank. The elderly driver was a Russian who spoke no English, but I was able to understand that the fare to Jerusalem would be one hundred and fifty shekels, which was about the right fare according to my earlier research. We set off in the early morning sunshine. The driver had programmed his SatNav system with my hotel address so he could find the hotel when we got to Jerusalem.

As we drove along the highway, floodgates of memories of the past opened. I marvelled at how much had changed in the country and yet how much had remained the same. The motorway pretty much followed the old route from thirty years before. My excitement increased as we started to wind our way up the hills into Jerusalem, passing familiar places like Shoresh and Abu Ghosh, places where we had gone to swim or for picnics as a family. I felt like that schoolboy from all those years ago coming home again! As we approached the suburbs of the city, I was reminded of the long-forgotten sight of metal barriers placed across certain roads cordoning off whole neighbourhoods. Of course, I had forgotten that it was Shabbat, the Jewish weekend. The orthodox Jewish community closed off their residential areas from dusk on Friday to dusk on Saturday. From memory, if you entered these areas driving, you ran the risk of being stoned or worse!

One of the more immediate problems with this was that the taxi's satellite navigation system didn't consider these cordoned-off neighbourhoods in trying to get us to my hotel. As a result, it kept trying to direct us down closed streets and the driver would have to try and find an alternative way round. It didn't help that the taxi driver was unfamiliar with the street network of Jerusalem, so we kept hitting dead ends. It was like the film Children of the Corn, where the couple in the car keep coming back to the same crossroads! Eventually, we finally made it to the city centre, but now we couldn't find my hotel as it was in a pedestrianised area. I rang the hotel and gave my phone to the driver to get directions to the closest place where he could drop me.

The hotel receptionist directed him to drop me at their sister hotel located around the corner, and they would send someone to walk me to my hotel. A few minutes later, we pulled up at the meeting point. As I unloaded my bag, the driver told me that the fare was three hundred shekels! I was not pleased with this, having agreed the fare at the airport, and proceeded to argue with him, me in English, he in a mix of Hebrew and Russian, until I finally gave in. Slapping my money into his outstretched hand, I stormed into the hotel to wait to be collected. This was not the return to the land of my birth that I had been looking forward to. The rose-tinted lenses that I had been wearing all these years had been swiftly swept away, and I quietly fumed at being so blatantly ripped off within the first few hours of my return.

As I waited, I sent several angry text messages to Pamela, somewhere over the Atlantic, warning her of what had happened with the taxi and our trip was probably now ruined before we had even started.

I was collected and led to my hotel, where I was disappointed to learn that my room would not be available until 1 pm, four hours away. Things were going from bad to worse.

The young receptionist asked me how my drive from Tel Aviv had been. I told her I was angry about being ripped off on the taxi fare. She asked me how much I had paid. When I told her she laughed and explained that taxi rates doubled when working over the Shabbat weekend. I had actually paid the correct fare! Feeling rather foolish, I quickly fired off more texts to Pamela telling her to ignore my earlier ranting messages.

With four hours to kill, I decided to take a walk and re-familiarize myself with the city. The area around my hotel remained much the same as I remembered, although I was disappointed that Richie's Pizza was no longer there. Richie's Pizza was an institution in our day, a regular stop off on the way home after a movie or night spent in the pub. One major change, however, was the new light rail network that ran through the middle of the now pedestrianised Jaffa Street down to Damascus Gate at the Old City and then on through French Hill, Beit Hanina (where we had lived) and on to the Israeli settlements in the West Bank. Another new feature was the shopping mall and walkway that extended from New Gate down to Jaffa Gate.

The streets were busy at this early hour, and I noticed that there were lots of people carrying palm fronds and wearing white robes. It transpired that our return to Jerusalem coincided with the Eastern Orthodox Church's Easter, and as a result the city was filled with Russians, Serbs, Greeks, Ethiopians, and others celebrating this important event. This day was apparently called the Day of Fire. I saw a large procession of pilgrims moving up from Jaffa Gate, many dressed in robes, banging drums, carrying pots of fire, and singing. It was all rather intoxicating as I stood watching: the sounds, the smells, the mix of faiths and outfits against the backdrop of the spectacularly walled Old City to my left and the famous King David Hotel and the YMCA dominating the skyline to my right. In the distance ahead was the Montefiore Windmill in the German Colony as I always remembered it, and there on a distant hill I could just make out the UN flag fluttering in the wind over Government House, the UN Headquarters where my father had worked all those years before.

Now I was excited at the prospect of the next four days as I took in all the familiar landmarks, and couldn't wait for Pamela to get here to share my excitement. I walked further down to Damascus Gate and then down Saladin Street, the main shopping street on the Arab side of the city.

I headed back to my hotel as the temperature began to rise and managed to doze on a couch in reception for a while before I was able to climb into my bed for a few hours of sleep when my room was finally ready.

I was woken by a call from Pamela later that afternoon as she checked in downstairs. I joined her in the lobby where she told me she had posted a message on Facebook saying how excited she was about going back to Jerusalem after thirty years. She had received a reply from John Chorlton, who had been the Principal of the Anglican Church International School in Jerusalem thirty years before. We had all attended the school at various times when we were children, and Pamela had still been a pupil there when my mother passed away in 1983. John was now a vicar based in Swindon in England. By pure coincidence, he happened to be visiting Jerusalem with his church group on the day we were arriving but was returning to the UK the next day! He had known Pamela and our mother well and hoped he could meet before they left the next day. Pamela had arranged to meet him and his wife that evening at the YMCA, a short walk from our hotel.

That evening, we set off towards the YMCA situated opposite the King David Hotel. As we passed by a petrol station we noticed a white SUV, with the familiar black UN initials painted on the side, parked in the forecourt. There was a man sitting in the passenger seat. Why not, I thought, and went over and asked if he would mind taking a photo of Pamela and me, standing beside the car. He was a little surprised by the request and asked why. I explained that thirty years before, our father had been the Chief Transport Officer for the UN in Jerusalem, responsible for all the UN vehicles like this one. Coming back after all these years there was a personal connection having our picture taken with the car. He was amused but agreed to take the picture, although whether he believed us or not was unclear; he probably thought that he needed to get rid of us quickly, who knows; but we had our picture taken, broad smiles on our faces.

We walked up the pathway to the YMCA, probably the most impressive YMCA you will find in the world in terms of architecture and location. We found John and his wife having dinner in one of the dining rooms. It was a very moving moment for them being thirty years since they had last met. John knew my mother well, and proceeded to recall stories about her that I had not heard before. The most poignant one was a story concerning a school concert. My mother had been sitting behind John, and at one point, she tapped him on the shoulder. When he turned around to her, she pointed hard at herself, then drew a line across her throat and pointed skywards. It was my mother's way of telling John that she was dying. I had to admire her sense of humour despite the difficult time she must have been going through.

We had a couple of beers together and shed a tear or two on the walk down memory lane, before John and his wife returned to their church group. It was a rewarding hour spent with the Chorltons and got our Jerusalem return off to the perfect start.

Chapter 17

The Old Neighbourhood

The next morning, we were up early and ready for the day ahead. Our plan was to visit the places that had a particular significance to us; our old house in the northern suburbs of Beit Hanina, Government House, the headquarters of the UN in the Middle East, the Anglican Church International School, Gethsemane, and the Old City.

After breakfast, we walked around the corner to Jaffa Street and boarded the light railway we needed to take out to Beit Hanina. We looked out the windows excitedly for familiar landmarks along the route however the city had undergone major changes over the preceding thirty years so at times we weren't sure of our location. When we passed through French Hill, we knew we were getting close to Beit Hanina and were the only ones to get off at the stop. I was delighted to see that we were opposite the apartment where our old friends the Connolly's had lived back then. We had spent many a Christmas night singing carols there with my mother playing along on the piano.

We had a long walk along the main road to get to the centre of Beit Hanina. After about three quarters of a mile, I recognized the road that led up to our old house. The girls' school was still there on the corner. We walked up the hill and there was the three-story building comprising six large apartments. It was exactly as we remembered it, albeit looking a little tired now and seemingly unoccupied for the most part. All the windows were covered with paper making it impossible to see inside. We were so excited at being back and immediately began taking lots of photos posing in front of the building. Our joy at being home however was suddenly interrupted when a man came out of the building shouting in Arabic, clearly angry about something.

We tried to explain as best we could, given the language difficulties, that we had lived in this house thirty years ago, but he didn't really understand. I then remembered that I had packed several old family photos and my dad's old UN passport in my rucksack. I dug them out and showed him the photos. There was a photo of my dad with Hosni, who used to clean the house and spend Christmas Day with us, sharing a beer. There was a family picture in the passport. I also had various pictures of Mark and Pamela. When he saw the photos, he calmed down, as it became clear he recognised us from those earlier years, although he seemed to think that there had been two girls in the family. Mark had long hair back then; we could only assume that he had thought Mark was a girl all along!

Although his attitude softened a little towards us,

he wouldn't allow us into the building, and went back inside. We took our final photos and walked back towards the main road. As we discussed the encounter, we realised that he must have been the son of the landlord at the time, who also lived in the building.

We headed a little further into Beit Hanina to the main crossroads. Down one of the roads was "Irish Alley" where many of the UN Irish families lived, but it was now a minor road dwarfed by a new motorway running parallel to it.

We found ourselves outside a teahouse and decided to go in for a cup of tea. We popped our heads inside the door and asked if it was okay to come in. There were a few men inside playing backgammon, smoking, and drinking sweet mint tea. They stopped and stared at us, dressed in our t-shirts and shorts, baseball caps and backpacks. Not the usual sight in Beit Hanina, I felt. One rose from his chair and welcomed us in. He spoke English, introducing himself as the owner. He then introduced us to his brother, sitting at a neighbouring table, who turned out to be the Mayor of Beit Hanina! They were curious to know who we were and why we were in the area. Mint tea and hummus were ordered as we explained what we were doing in Beit Hanina.

To our surprise, the owner remembered the Irish families who had lived in the neighbourhood back then. In fact, his parents had owned several houses which had been rented out to UN families; he even remembered the Mooney family! He told us that the building we lived in had previously been the headquarters of the Palestinian Liberation

Organisation, the PLO, up to 1967. He also confirmed our suspicion that the man we had met earlier was the son of our old landlord. He commented that the man was a bit majnoon—crazy in the head.

We mentioned how he had reacted to our taking photos outside the building. The mayor explained that there was an ongoing game of cat and mouse being played between the Israelis and Palestinians over illegal land development, as seen by the Israelis, and illegal land seizures, as seen by the Palestinians. Israeli agents would often appear in the area, dressed like we were, taking photos of "illegal" buildings, and he had probably suspected we were the same.

He said that we were probably quite lucky that the situation hadn't escalated further. On a different day, we might have attracted an angry crowd with unforeseen consequences.

We spent a fun hour reminiscing and taking photos with the owner and the mayor, but the time came for us to bid our farewells and we reluctantly set off back to the tram stop, congratulating ourselves on our morning's success and looking forward to the next stage of our odyssey.

Chapter 18

Walking Down Memory Lane

We jumped off the tram at Damascus Gate and walked into the Old City. Experiencing the Old City is to take a step back in time. The Jewish, Muslim, Christian, and Armenian Quarters are all contained within the walls of the Old City. You could be walking through the narrow streets of the Muslim Quarter, and its shops selling a mix of spices, t-shirts, keffiyehs and souvenirs of Jerusalem; take a right turn, and suddenly find yourself in the Christian Quarter with its rosary beads, crosses, and all manner of religious icons!

We had lunch and then set off to explore. We headed into the Christian Quarter. As it was the Eastern Orthodox Easter weekend our way was crowded with pilgrims following the Stations of the Cross along the Via Dolorosa, but we finally found ourselves at the Church of the Holy Sepulchre, where Jesus was reputedly laid to rest after his crucifixion, one of the holiest sites in Jerusalem for Christians.

The Church has always been shared and managed on

a rotating basis by the various Christian faiths, Roman Catholic, Greek Orthodox, Eastern Orthodox and Armenian, resulting in centuries old disputes between the different faiths. The smallest perceived slight or disagreement could often lead to brawls between the clergy of the different faiths. On this special occasion, the Church was crowded with pilgrims, many waiting for their turn to kneel at and kiss the stone where Jesus was laid. We managed to make our way inside and spent some time taking in the incredible architecture. At one point, a single shaft of sunlight suddenly descended through a hole in the ceiling high above illuminating the spot below. It was surreal and almost mystical, perfectly capturing the occasion.

We carried on exploring the narrow streets of the Old City before heading back to our hotel. The receptionist at our hotel was fascinated by our trip. We were not the usual tourists in the traditional sense in that we were visiting areas of the city that Israelis and tourists would not normally visit. We recounted our visit to Beit Hanina and were surprised by her reaction when I mentioned that our old house had been the headquarters of the PLO.

She said, "What's the PLO?"

I was perplexed at this and realised that her generation had grown up hearing and reading only of the Palestinian groups Fatah and Hamas. The PLO in the context that we remembered it was rarely if ever mentioned any more.

Our evening recollections were also appreciated by an elderly American couple visiting Israel for the first time. They were amazed to hear of our background and itinerary and lapped up our daily stories. It was particularly amusing one day when the wife asked me if I thought it would be safe to walk around the city the next day as she had heard on the news that Israel had fired some missiles into Syria. I recounted my experience of Kinshasa back in 1993 during the Second Pillage where I had not felt in danger and had been evacuated to the UK, only to be mugged at knifepoint in London! My philosophy therefore was "wrong place, wrong time, it doesn't matter where you are" so I wouldn't personally be concerned.

"I like your attitude," she exclaimed and turning to her husband, announced confidently that they were going out the next day.

Before travelling to Israel, we had contacted the youngest daughter of old Irish friends of my parents who had lived and worked in Jerusalem and the UN during our time. Rachel now lived in Jerusalem working for the UN herself, so we wanted to use the opportunity to see a familiar face again. We had grown up with Rachel's brothers and sisters, and we looked forward to catching up with her again after all these years. To our delight, Rachel told us that her mother Theresa was also visiting Jerusalem from Ireland the very same weekend we were in Jerusalem. We would meet her for dinner that night.

Our second evening at Jerusalem, we took a taxi to Rachel's and had an emotional reunion with her mother. The old photo albums came out, and over too many bottles of wine we recalled many happy memories from thirty years ago and more. It was a magical evening, although one could guess that the hangover the next day was not going to be a good one.

We were keen to find the church where our parents had married. We had a photo with us taken on their wedding day with my parents standing by a car in front of an alley in the Old City. Rachel's husband was able to tell us exactly where it was taken and where the church in relation to it was. The church we were looking for was called the Church of Our Saviour. He even remarked that the photo had been developed by a well-known photographer in Jerusalem at the time.

Rachel surprised us further by informing us that she had arranged passes for us to visit the UN Headquarters at Government House the next morning. We would be collected in the morning at the YMCA by someone who had worked with our dad all those years ago.

The next morning, we made our way, a little gingerly, to the YMCA. Soon, a Toyota Landcruiser with UN markings pulled in, and we were introduced to our guide, Said Jarallah. He was an elderly Palestinian with a ready sense of humour, and we warmed to each other immediately. He was rather scathing of the UN in Jerusalem today, complaining that security at the main gate was lax and outsourced to a private local company. The road leading to the main entrance was now an obstacle course of concrete barriers to deter car bombs, a sad sign of the times we lived in. We handed over our ID documents at the security gate and entered the compound for the first time in thirty years.

It felt like time had turned back as we entered. We drove over to the garages and workshops of the transport section where our father had been in charge all those years ago. The old Post Exchange or PX as it was known was still there, now with a coffee bar outside and in front of us were the same metal stairs leading up to my father's office on the top floor of the transport offices. Nothing appeared to have really changed at all.

We walked towards the main building with its grand arched entrance and circular drive surrounding a sunken garden. As kids we had used that circular drive as our own running track seeing who could post the fastest time for a lap.

Growing up, we had spent a lot of time at Government House. We would go up there during the week to shop at the PX for items not readily available in the local shops, play tennis, see our father, and have lunch in the restaurant. Practically every Sunday, if we were not in Gaza for the weekend at the beach club, the Irish families would head up to Government House for lunch after Mass at Gethsemane. These lunches would generally turn into a long afternoon drinking session for our parents whilst we were left to fend for ourselves, to play football on the lawns at the back or hide and seek. Inevitably boredom would set in, and we would return to the dining room and want to go home. We were usually fobbed off by our parents with the "we'll be going after we finish this beer" just as Speedy, the waiter, came flying out of the kitchen bearing yet another tray laden with bottles of Heineken, whiskey, and wine!

As a result, particularly in our younger years, the Irish kids, and there were a lot of us, caused all manner of trouble for our parents at Government House. We particularly enjoyed seeing who could climb highest on the huge electricity pylon located in the grounds. On another occasion we came across rows of Jeep Cherokees parked on the outer boundary of the UN compound. It just seemed a very good idea at the time to throw stones at them and see if we could break their windscreens. By the time we had finished, we had smashed every window, and departed the scene feeling satisfied with ourselves.

The following Monday, our fathers were summoned by the General in charge and given a severe dressing down over the incident, and no doubt warned to keep their feral kids under control or face the consequences. It turned out that the Jeeps had been sold to a local car dealer and we had gone and destroyed every window! I think our dads were extremely lucky not to have been fired that day. Our parents weren't averse to using the wooden spoon or belt strap if needed, and I suspect we all felt the slap of leather or wood on our backsides that night.

Walking into Government House itself brought all these memories back, the Sunday lunches, our parents' twenty-fifth wedding anniversary dinner in the dining room, the New Year's Eve party in the ballroom, the mysterious staircase at the end of the hall leading up to the General's quarters. As it was Sunday, the building was quiet with only a few military personnel sitting in the dining room. It seemed the kitchen no longer opened on a Sunday, so we bought some coffees and sat out on the terrace.

Said recounted stories of what it was like working with the Irish in Government House. The Irish achieved a certain notoriety in their time for partying hard. By all accounts the St Patrick's Day party in the Mount Scopus Hotel in Jerusalem was the party to be invited to; even the General, it seemed, was keen to get on the invite list. There is a photograph taken in Gaza on St Patrick's Day in 1958, capturing all the Irish couples in their black tie and gowns looking extremely glamorous. If ever a photo showed just how the lives of the Irish had changed for the better, in the space of twelve months, then that photo was it.

Our host recalled how some of the Irish men would sometimes sneak off to a quiet room in the morning with files under their arms for a "meeting", as a ruse to have a few beers or perhaps something stronger. Said was a Christian and drank alcohol so he was often invited along too. The Irish would tell him they were going for a "green banana", their code word for a bottle of Heineken!

There were occasions when one of the Irish men would drive home with a little too much green banana in him and end up with a bump or scrape to his official car. The next day he would have to come in and face my father, sheepishly explaining what happened in the hope that my father would okay the repairs in the workshop. My father would apparently wag his finger and reprimand the unfortunate soul and tell them not to do it again, before signing off on the repairs.

I remember some of those dads, including my own, got well and truly oiled and it's a miracle none were killed driving home. Unfortunately for some, the booze took over their lives and made for some unhappy home experiences. When one takes away the rosy tinted glasses, for many, the reality of life was that alcohol played a big part in their day-to-day home life and not always for the best.

My own father had his own problems with alcohol in the years before he retired, likely brought about by the realisation that my mother was dying. With hindsight, he was fifty-four when she died, and having reached that age myself, I now understand how difficult it must have been to deal with it, and understand what he must have been going through inside. Whilst I don't condone how he acted then; I can understand it now.

After we finished our coffee, we strolled through the gardens towards the tennis courts and then back to the workshop offices where it was time to head off on the next leg. As we left Government House, we were handed back our ID documents. Except Pamela was given the ID documents of an Israeli woman! The security team had mixed up Pamela's ID with an Israeli one and given hers to someone else! Said rolled his eyes and said it just proved how things had gotten worse in Government House since our time there. Pamela's ID, her driving licence, was eventually returned to her in the US.

We were driven to the Mount of Olives with its stunning view across to the Old City and the golden domed Al Aqsa Mosque. Below us was the Church of Gethsemane. This was where we attended Mass every Sunday, where we had received our first Holy Communion and Confirmation. Gethsemane was always a fascinating place and I had strong memories of it; the arrival of the Irish families in their Sunday best trying to find parking in the narrow street outside, the ever present Palestinian tour guides with their camels touting for business, the walk along the garden path into the dark church, waiting for your eyes to acclimatise to the pitch dark before picking a folding chair out of the side wall and finding a place to sit. Mass was always consecrated by Father Godfrey, an American priest, using the natural acoustics of the church to project his deep voice. It always amused me that during Mass, busloads of tourists would be walking around the church with their tour guide, taking photos of the mosaics and paintings, and chattering away sotto voce.

Today. Gethsemane felt much smaller than I remembered. The main front entrance, never open in our time, was now the only way in rather than the side entrance we had used. There were major renovations being undertaken inside but the place was as busy as ever with tourists and of course, a Mass was being said at the time. So not much had really changed!

At this point we bade a fond farewell to Said and jumped into a taxi to head back to Damascus Gate in search of the church where our parents had married. The Palestinian taxi drivers would always assume we were the usual tourists visiting the city. We would point out we had in fact been born in East Jerusalem and had lived for many years in Beit Hanina. They would be surprised but only really believed us when I produced my birth certificate issued by the Royal Hashemite Kingdom of Jordan stating my place of birth as Saint Joseph's Hospital, Beit Hanina, Jerusalem, written in English and Arabic. One taxi driver, on seeing this, proclaimed that we were brothers!

At Damascus Gate we headed back into the narrow streets of the Old City and worked our way along the Via Dolorosa again and then through several side streets until we came upon the Church of Our Saviour. I was struck by how beautiful it was inside but oddly I had no recollection of ever being taken there in my youth; and jokingly wondered if perhaps in later years they had regretted getting married and couldn't bear to be reminded of it by visiting the church.

Next door was the College des Freres, the parish office, so we went in and introduced ourselves at the reception. We explained why we were visiting Jerusalem and asked them if they might have the original record of our parent's marriage.

The receptionist called a monk over who asked us when they had married.

"1957," I replied, showing him a copy of the marriage certificate.

"Oh, that should be easy," he said, "Our records go back centuries!"

And taking my copy of the marriage certificate he disappeared down a corridor. After a short wait he returned with a ledger in one hand and some papers in the other. He opened the ledger to July 1957 and there was my parents' marriage licence in full, including the details of our Irish grandparents who had died when we were very young, and the witnesses to the marriage. The monk also pointed out that the priest who had officiated at the wedding had been a very senior priest in the Vatican hierarchy at that time. It would have been a huge honour for my parents to have been married by him! He then handed us copies of the full marriage licence as a keepsake.

Leaving the College des Freres, we retraced our steps and came across the exact spot where my parents had been photographed on their wedding day in 1957. Nothing had changed since; the narrow alley behind, the garage door on their left was still there, as was the shop on the right. Holding the original photo taken in 1957, Pamela and I recreated that picture and had our photo taken in the same spot.

Chapter 19

Closing the Circle

Our third day saw us heading off to visit our old school, The Anglican Church International School. I had been at school there till the age of twelve, before being sent back to a boarding school in Ireland in 1975. Pamela had attended until 1983, before coming back to Ireland when our father retired. Pamela had somehow managed to get the contact details of a teacher at the school and had arranged for us to be able to visit, so we were expected.

My first impression as we walked up the street was that the height of the school walls had been raised quite substantially since our time, another sign of the enhanced security requirements of the day. We were admitted into the main office building and were surprised to find a small museum section there, celebrating the history of the school and its role as a hospital before that. Canice, our eldest brother, had been born in the hospital in 1958, whilst the rest of us had gone to the school after it was converted from a hospital.

The museum celebrated the European benefactors of the hospital and the British and Irish Jewish community who had contributed towards the establishment of the hospital and its upkeep. I noticed a beautiful marble fountain piece which had been donated by a family from County Carlow in Ireland in the 1800s.

Pamela's contact, Anne Brunskill, arrived and asked us to wait in the library until classes broke up for lunch, after which we were free to walk around the school grounds at our leisure. We sat in the library and browsed through old yearbooks we found dating back to the 1980s. We made some small entertainment for ourselves by finding photos of many of our old classmates, photographing them, and posting them on Facebook later for amusement.

Finally, the lunch bell sounded, and we strolled around the school, each of us with our own personal memories of our time here. The middle school, which I had attended, was unchanged, with the windows of the classrooms still sporting the same green painted wooden shutters; the basketball court was the same, and the black faded outline of a goal was still painted onto the school wall, exactly where it had been thirty or more years previously.

It was fascinating to walk around, lost in our own memories of our school days; in my case: assembly at the start of day, the spelling tests (which I invariably won!); performing The Hobbit, with myself as Bilbo Baggins, of course, learning seventeen pages of script; the great classmates of Middle 3, my last year in

1975: Judi Axelbank, Lois Nastoff, Lydia Doric, Mick O'Connor, Brendan Mullin (who went on to become one of Ireland's top rugby star's), Danny MacCaffery, Alex Wiedl, Pakpong Rochanaprok, Ben Schlessinger (the class comedian), John Monson, Rogelio Santos, and of course our amazing English teacher Ms Hall, the memories were endless!

When it was time to go, we headed back to the main office to thank Anne for arranging our visit. As an afterthought I asked her if she was any relation to David Brunskill. Quite surprised by my question, she confirmed that he was indeed her father and asked how I knew him. I explained that I had worked with him for many years at Grindlays Bank back in the 1990s. A small world indeed, we agreed, although I didn't have the heart to tell her that he was known as "Numbskull" Brunskill for his lack of tact and diplomacy generally.

I also complimented her on the interesting museum section at the school but expressed some surprise at the contribution Côte d'Ivoire had made in its early years. She was a little confused and asked what I meant. I pointed out that the section celebrating the British and Irish contribution to the hospital had the Union Jack and the flag of Côte d'Ivoire in the display rather than the Irish flag; the difference being the flag of Côte d'Ivoire is the reverse of the Irish flag. They were in fact displaying the orange, white, and green colours of Côte d'Ivoire!

She was mortified and said that the flags had been on display for years now without anyone ever mentioning it! She would have to get it put right! We felt that this was probably an appropriate time to leave, and so with a final farewell we left her staring at the display and shaking her head in bemusement.

Our final objective was to find Saint Joseph's Hospital in Sheikh Jarrah. The hospital had a particularly poignant connection for us as we were both born there. We always attended midnight mass in the chapel there every Christmas Eve with the other Irish families, and more recently our mother had passed away in the hospital in 1983. Christmas Eve midnight mass was always a fun occasion. It usually started with us teenagers heading off to Champs Pub in town for a few pre-Christmas beers to celebrate before meeting up with our parents at the hospital. They would always be concerned that we might be drunk when we turned up, but we were usually just a little tipsy and giggly. This didn't help once the mass started. The Irish nuns working at the hospital would play a cassette of Christmas carols on an old cassette player. Unfortunately, the batteries in the cassette player always seemed to be about to die. Combine the tone-deaf singing of the nuns, a cassette that frequently changed speed, our own lamentable attempts to join in the singing with a few pints in us, and you had the perfect ingredients for the frequent giggling fits that broke out throughout mass, interspersed with stern looks from our parents.

Now, we arrived at the hospital and asked if we could visit the chapel. The receptionist was a little surprised by our request and directed us to the hospital administrator's office. We explained the reason for our visit, showing him copies of our birth certificates and my mother's death certificate issued by the hospital. He was only too happy to comply with our request.

We were shown to the chapel on the top floor and were amazed at how much bigger the room looked now to how we remembered it as teenagers. We were amused to see that the old cassette recorder had finally gone and in its place was now a modern ghetto blaster, plugged in to a power socket!

Having taken a few moments' reflection and quietly offering a prayer to our mum, we decided that it was time to treat ourselves to lunch. And for us, what better place was there than the American Colony Hotel down the road in the American Colony! The American Colony Hotel had a particular significance to us; it was the top hotel for visiting dignitaries when in Jerusalem. We always passed it when we were living there but had never been inside or used its facilities, as it was too expensive then. Now we had the opportunity to go and treat ourselves to lunch and raise a "green banana" to all our friends and family! The hotel was everything we believed it would be, a tranquil oasis in the city where we enjoyed a few green bananas and a club sandwich. I always judge a hotel by its club sandwich, and this was up there at the top.

After lunch, we walked back to the Old City and walked along the ramparts of the city walls taking in a final perspective of the city. We took photos of the key landmarks before heading into the Armenian

Quarter for one final act. The quarter was known for its ceramic pottery, and Pamela wanted to buy some gifts to bring back to the US.

We went into a shop and whilst Pamela was busy looking at the ceramics, I started talking to the owner. He was about my age and, as with all the other people we had met on the trip, interested to know what we were doing in Jerusalem. I casually mentioned that I had known an Armenian girl all those years ago called Sylvia. The owner looked at me and exclaimed "You know Sylvia?"

He explained that Sylvia's family were extremely well known in Armenian circles. Her uncle had been the Armenian Archbishop in Jerusalem, one of the highest-ranking posts in the Armenian Church. The shop owner had lost touch with her family and wondered where Sylvia and her sister were now. I was able to tell him that Sylvia was settled in Paris and her sister in New York, and both were doing well. He was delighted to hear the news and when we departed, he presented me with a gift of a ceramic tile of the Jerusalem Cross, which now hangs in my house.

Having spent three days in Jerusalem, it was time to head home. We had one last day, so we decided to head to Tel Aviv where we sat on the beach, enjoying the warm sand and sun, basking in the recollection of our time spent in Jerusalem and the amazing coincidences that had brought us together with so many people who had connections to our old life. It was magical to return and revisit old haunts, to post photos on Facebook for our absent UN friends around the world, to be able to share in our journey. Jerusalem was a wonderful city to visit with its incredible history that linked into our own personal history. It was either pure luck or some greater power intervened that allowed us to visit the places we did on both sides of the city in a period of calm and tranquillity.

Ultimately, it felt good to finally close the circle, to lay to rest, once and for all, the ghost that had haunted me for thirty years. I couldn't have done it without my sister, Pamela, to whom I am eternally grateful for joining me. The next time I came back, I vowed it would be with my family. I have no doubt they would be as impressed with the experience as I was.

I headed to the airport that evening, boarded my flight for London and settled into my seat, finally at peace with myself and ready to move forward.

Over the years, there have been plenty of other interesting and amusing experiences in my life, plenty of travails during my travels, you might say, but these are the ones that have made such a lasting impression on me. I always thought it a shame that my own father did not record his own unique experiences, exciting and dangerous no doubt, during his nearly thirty years with the United Nations in Gaza, Israel, Egypt, Syria, and Pakistan at the heart of many major world crises and wars in that time.

Perhaps one day I will collect the stories from his surviving peers and put together another collection of memories for posterity.

I have loved my travels and travails over the years in Africa and the experiences that came with them. I always felt immediately at home wherever I landed and never once felt personally at risk. I believe that is a testament to my parents and their own decision to move overseas in the late 1950s. That decision exposed me to many different cultures, religions, races, and creeds growing up; it allowed me to travel to all manner of countries confident that whatever environment I happened to find myself in at the time, I would be at ease in it.

But at the end of it all, I hope that this series of recollections goes some way to providing my own children with a sense of the fun and variety of the world beyond their own borders. I hope that it might one day instil in them the same desire and confidence their grandfather and I had to take a risk and venture out to experience the world and all it has to offer for themselves.

THE END

Printed in Great Britain
by Amazon

39854338R00101